The
Guardian
Guide
to the
Economy

The Guardian Guide to the Economy

Frances Cairncross and Phil Keeley

Methuen
London and New York

First published in 1981 by
Methuen & Co. Ltd
11 New Fetter Lane, London EC4P 4EE
Published in the USA by
Methuen & Co.
in association with Methuen, Inc.
733 Third Avenue, New York, NY 10017
Reprinted 1982

Typeset in Great Britain by
Scarborough Typesetting Services
and printed by
Richard Clay (The Chaucer Press) Ltd
Bungay, Suffolk

British Library Cataloguing in Publication Data

Cairncross, Frances
The Guardian guide to the economy.
1. Great Britain − Economic conditions − 1945 −
I. Title   II. Keeley, Phil
330.9′41′058   HC256.6

ISBN 0 416 32560 2
ISBN 0 416 32570 X Pbk
ISBN 0 423 50940 3 Lp

Contents

Introduction

There was once a book review which began 'This work fills a much needed gap'. The gap this book is meant to fill is the one between the economic textbook and the daily newspaper. Anyone without a formal education in economics who takes a lively interest in the political debate is likely to be stumped, from time to time, by coming across an issue or a term whose significance is clearly much greater than can be explained in a short article. On the other hand, anyone who approaches economics by studying it in a textbook may sometimes find it difficult to see the relevance of the theory to current debates among politicians.

So this is not a description of how the economy works. It is an explanation of the main economic problems which Britain appears to face at the start of the 1980s. It attempts to give some flavour of the political argument over these problems – over import controls, for instance, or over the importance of monetary policy. It also tries to bring out the practical problems: the difficulties of controlling public spending, for example, or of alleviating poverty without destroying incentives.

The chapters in Part One grew out of a series of 'Economics Teach-Ins' written by Frances Cairncross run in *The Guardian* in 1980–1. We are grateful to *The Guardian* for permission to revise and use the material. To make the book more useful for school teachers of economics, Part Two contains worksheets devised by Phil Keeley relevant to each chapter and built around questions appropriate to 'A' level and BEC. These may

vii

look intimidating if you are an ordinary reader. Do not worry: you do not need to be able to follow them in order to understand the main body of the book. Just be grateful that you do not have to take an examination in 'A' level economics. . . .

FRANCES CAIRNCROSS
PHIL KEELEY

PART ONE

1 Running the economy: how much does money matter?

Much of the debate in British economics today is presented to the public in terms of two contrasting schools of thought: as an argument between monetarists and Keynesians. The contrast is often overdone. To label economists in this way is to caricature the subject. But there are discernible differences of approach and this chapter is an attempt to pick them out and to explain them.

In doing so, it inevitably exaggerates. Economics is a large and complex territory, and two economists who might both be described as 'monetarist' by their critics might subscribe to surprisingly different beliefs. Neither monetarism nor Keynesianism has a set of 'Thirty Nine Articles', like the Anglican Church, against which the orthodoxy of believers can be measured.

There is also an element of caricature – or at least of considerable simplification – in the way that some of the economic relationships are described in this chapter. It is no accident that the pages of economic journals tend to be rolling meadows of algebra, through which meanders a thin rivulet of text. Algebra happens to be a neater and more precise way of explaining how economists think of the links in the mechanism of the economy than plain words. Words can be made to do the job, but at considerably greater length.

Keynesianism is a relatively new way of looking at the economy. It is named after a British economist: John Maynard Keynes. Keynes wrote his most famous work – *The General*

Theory of Employment, Interest and Money (1936)[1] – at the time of the Great Depression, a period when prices actually fell. Not surprisingly, Keynesian economists have been more preoccupied with the problems of growth and of the management of demand and the level of unemployment than with the problem of rising prices. They have also tended to regard fiscal policy – the balance of government spending and government borrowing – as the main instrument of economic policy. Keynesianism has been the dominant influence on the post-war generation of politicians, government officials and economists, particularly in Britain.

Monetarism, by contrast, is a much older way of looking at the economy. Indeed, in its simplest form, it must be one of the oldest ideas in economics. Its core is the belief that there is a stable and predictable link between the amount of money in the economy and the level of prices. Its main preoccupation is inflation – and monetarists rely fundamentally on monetary policy to cure inflation.

Monetarism was formalized by an American economist, Irving Fisher, although its origins lie in the work of the eighteenth-century Scots economist, David Hume. Fisher was an extraordinary man. He was one of the leading members of the American prohibitionist party. For thirty years or so he interviewed all potential presidential candidates to discover their views on the subject of alcohol. He was also a statistician and mathematician of some distinction. He invented the Kardex filing system, and founded what later became the Remington-Rand Corporation to produce and market it.

He also developed what became known as the 'Quantity Theory of Money' equation. This equation, $MV = PT$, is a shorthand way of saying that money (M) multiplied by the velocity (V) at which it circulates equals the level of prices (P) multiplied by the volume of transactions (T). In other words, the amount of money in the economy must be enough to finance the total value of all economic activity.

For the first three decades of this century, the conventional view of how prices, output and employment were determined in

[1] All references are given in full in the bibliography.

any economy was based on Fisher's equation and the analysis behind it. It was generally thought that the velocity of circulation — the speed with which a given amount of money worked its way around the economy — was on the whole fairly stable. This was important: if the velocity fluctuated widely there would obviously be some circumstances in which the same level of economic activity could be financed with much less money in the economy than at other times.

Because velocity was thought to be relatively stable, it was believed that changes in the quantity of money — the money supply, as we would now call it — would explain changes in output and in prices. Most people thought that in the medium term, the trend of prices would reflect the behaviour of the quantity of money. In the short term, monetary policy was regarded as the main instrument for stabilizing the economy. In particular, changes in interest rates were regarded as the way of slowing down the economy if prices were rising sharply; or of stimulating the demand for goods and services if the economy was flagging and unemployment rising.

Then came the Great Depression. To most observers, it appeared that monetary policy had failed. It was unable to revive the economy. Interest rates had been cut as far as they could be cut. This meant that the possibilities of using monetary policy to try to stimulate the economy had been exhausted.

Interest rates, argued Keynes, would not solve the problem of inadequate demand. It was perfectly possible to reach a position where interest rates were so low that everyone expected them to rise. In that situation, everyone would hang on to their cash, waiting for rates to rise. If the government tried to expand economic activity by expanding the amount of money in the economy, the money would simply disappear into holdings of cash. Investment would remain stagnant.

The central dilemma, as Keynes identified it, was that the economy was not necessarily self-adjusting. It might get stuck at a high level of unemployment, simply because there were not enough investment opportunities to absorb the savings which people were making. At that point, savings might well be equal to investment, but at a level of output which was unacceptably low.

3

Fisher's famous equation, said Keynes, had been wrongly interpreted. The velocity at which money circulated was not stable — far from it. It could change for a number of reasons: it might fall if the money supply was rising, for instance, or it might rise if incomes were increasing. The inflexible bit of the equation, said Keynes, was prices. They were determined by costs. Costs in turn were determined mainly by money wages — by what people were paid. Wages in turn could not easily be changed, or at least reduced.

That meant that prices were much less flexible downwards than output. Keynes re-directed attention to the relationships between incomes, spending, saving, output and investment. One of the points in his thought which later economists have built on is the concept of the multiplier. If individuals acquired an increase in income, he pointed out, they were unlikely to spend the whole of it. Some would be saved. The extra expenditure would represent more demand and lead to more new jobs and more new income — and again, a small part would be saved. Ultimately, the process would exhaust itself. It was a way of pointing out that the effects of an increase or decrease in government spending had a ripple effect across the whole economy.

Thus Keynes identified the cause of the Great Depression as a collapse of investment, which in turn caused a collapse of income, which fed back again into yet lower investment. Lower interest rates would not re-start the engine. Keynes's cure was essentially that the government should borrow those savings which business did not want to borrow and invest, and should increase public sector investment instead. That would raise incomes — and so demand — and start the economy moving again.

Now this view of the world has had a massive influence on post-war economic policy in many industrial countries, in spite of the fact that for the first twenty-five years after the Second World War the main problem of economic policy was usually too many investment projects chasing too little savings, rather than the other way around. Keynes's work was interpreted to mean that monetary policy was of little importance. It could not be used to keep the economy ticking over at a high level of output and employment. That was essentially the job of fiscal policy — government spending and taxation. Interest rates thus became a subordinate instrument of policy: instead of trying to influence economic activity by varying the level of interest rates, the government's job was to keep them as low as possible, in order to hold down the cost of public sector borrowing, and to create a favourable climate for business investment.

A further important implication was that inflation was largely the result of rising costs — for which read rising wages. That in turn gave Keynesian economic policies their preoccupation with unemployment, and later their emphasis on incomes policies to deal with inflation.

In the second half of the 1960s, this orthodoxy began to be questioned. The Irving Fisher of our generation is Milton Friedman: not as versatile as his predecessor, but every bit as persuasive. Friedman has long held a chair in economics at Chicago University. He is diminutive, highly articulate, and as the recent television series 'Free to Choose' (on which his book, *Free to Choose*, is based) demonstrated, he is a highly effective popularizer.

Friedman, after a massive review of economic history, came to the conclusion that inflation was 'always and everywhere a monetary phenomenon'. He argued that a change in the money supply would show up, after about six to nine months, in a change in output. Six to nine months later, that is succeeded by a change in the rate of rise of prices.* In the first Wincott Lecture (*The Counter-Revolution in Monetary Theory*, 1970) he set out the following propositions:

In the short run, which may be as much as five or ten years, monetary changes affect primarily output. Over decades, on the other hand, the rate of monetary growth affects primarily prices. . . . Inflation . . . is and can be produced only by a more rapid increase in the quantity of money than in output. Government spending may or may not be inflationary. It clearly will be inflationary if it is financed by creating money, that is, by printing currency or creating bank deposits. . . . Fiscal policy is extremely important in determining what fraction of total national income is spent by government and who bears the burden

* Asterisks indicate that a relevant question can be found in Part Two.

of that expenditure. By itself, it is not important for inflation.

(Friedman, 1970; 23–4)

Since Friedman first raised the banner of the monetarist counter-revolution, the ground between most monetarists and most Keynesians has narrowed. For instance, monetarists have, by and large, come to acknowledge that inflation may be a more complex phenomenon than they first argued, and that both trade unions and fiscal policy may have a more direct effect on inflation than Friedman's blunt statement would suggest. Keynesians, for their part, would mostly acknowledge that an increase in the money supply may create the conditions for faster inflation, even if it does not directly cause it.

But there are still some very important areas of debate. Some of them underlie the current debate on economic policy. In the remainder of this chapter, I want to look first at the way in which monetarists tend to think that money affects the economy, and to contrast it with the Keynesian view. Then I want to briefly look at the history of monetary policy, and at the difficulties both in controlling what actually happens to money and in making monetary policy influence the inflation rate. As I said at the start of this chapter, the whole task is complicated by the fact that a fairly disparate crew of economists marches under each flag, even in Britain alone. There is a considerable difference between the sort of severe monetarism put forward by Patrick Minford of Liverpool University and the more gradualist policies advocated by Alan Budd at the London Business School. Similarly, there are plenty of economists who would regard themselves as Keynesians, but who recoil in alarm from the views of the Cambridge Economic Policy Group (CEPG) and its director Wynne Godley. But here goes.

Monetarists believe that in the medium term, the government has a powerful influence on the rate of inflation but very little on the underlying rate of growth, and none at all on the underlying rate of unemployment. The level of unemployment – so most monetarists would argue – is not directly under the government's control in anything but the short run. There is a 'natural' rate of unemployment. This is a confusing phrase – it tends to mean different things to different economists. But in

6

this context, it refers to the concept of a level of unemployment at which inflation will not accelerate. That natural or underlying rate of unemployment can only be altered by measures which affect the structure of the job market: thus a cut in the level of unemployment benefit might make people spend less time looking for a new job, and might make them more prepared to take a job that paid less. That would bring down the 'natural' rate of unemployment. The job market is ultimately a market like any other, monetarists would argue. Wages reflect the supply of, and demand for, labour. If trade unions artificially push up wages beyond the rates at which supply and demand are matched, they will reduce the demand for labour − or in other words, cause unemployment.

If the government tries to pursue Keynesian policies and to push the level of unemployment down below its natural rate, it will succeed in the short run. But the short run will get shorter and shorter. For the tools of Keynesian demand stimulation − more government spending or lower taxes − call for more government borrowing. And unless the economy is very depressed, more government borrowing will almost certainly mean faster monetary growth.

As a government policy of expansion begins to take effect − so monetarists would argue − the first result will be a rise in output. People will have more money to spend: factories will have more demand to satisfy. But as the months go by, businessmen will start to outbid each other in the scramble to find workers, or raw materials, or components. Prices will start to rise faster. The shortages will kill off the expansion (or government policy will be hastily thrown into reverse). The economy will fall back to its old growth rate − or below it − but with a faster rate of inflation. The reason is that while it is relatively easy for output growth to be reduced, inflation, once it has started, seems to become ingrained in the economy.*

That is one view of the way in which the creation of more money puts up prices. But monetarists argue among themselves about the 'transmission mechanism'. Since the advent of flexible exchange rates in the early 1970s, there has been an increasingly popular argument that the link runs through the exchange rate. If monetary growth in Britain is faster than monetary growth

7

elsewhere, the result will be an outflow of money across the exchanges. The exchange rate will fall — and that will push up the price of imported goods. That in turn will create pressures for pay rises which will eventually offset most or all of the gains in competitiveness won by the falling exchange rate. The result at the end of the day will be the same: faster inflation, no faster growth.

To slow down inflation, monetarists argue, you simply slow down the rate of excess monetary growth. Some say you have to slow it down quickly, some that you have to slow it down gradually. All accept that the initial effect is likely to be a sharp rise in the level of unemployment, as the drop in output precedes the drop in the inflation rate.* Ultimately, the money supply ought to grow no faster than the rate of output, or a little faster if governments are prepared to accept a little inflation.

For how long and to what levels unemployment rises will depend basically on how fast wages adjust. If workers are prepared to accept a drop in living standards for a while, then they will price themselves back into work quite quickly. Monetarists accept that this will be deeply painful, and those who argue for bringing monetary growth down quickly do so mainly because they doubt whether the nerve of governments will hold if unemployment remains high and rising for more than a few years.

The whole process may be speeded up, monetarists argue, if people can be brought to expect that the inflation rate will fall and to change their wage demands accordingly. It is important, they say, to change people's expectations — the faster people expect inflation to come down, the less painful the process will be. That is part of the logic for setting targets for monetary growth. Targets are supposed to make it plain to everyone that the government is really determined to bring down monetary growth. It might also be an argument for using incomes policy to put a brake on pay rises — though monetarists do not usually like incomes policy much.

Once inflation has been brought down, monetarists argue that unemployment will come down too — without the need for government stimulus. For as inflation comes down, it will be possible to reduce interest rates — high interests rates tend to be the inevitable mechanism by which monetary growth is choked

8

off. As inflation and interest rates come down, monetarists argue, people will save less (and so spend more) and companies will be more willing to borrow for investment. There are, in other words, powerful self-stabilizing forces in the economy.

Now what of the Keynesian counter-arguments? There are two of particular importance. First, Keynesians believe that wages are determined largely by prices and are not, initially at least, affected by the state of the job market. Second, they are more sceptical than monetarists about the ability of the government to control the rate at which the money supply grows. Indeed, they tend to view the money supply in a completely different light from monetarists: more as a reflection of what is happening in the economy, and less as an instrument of policy in the government's hands.

To expand the first of these points: in spite of a very large increase in unemployment in the past decade, Keynesians would argue, there has been precious little sign that wages respond to market forces. Wages are highly influenced by trade unions, and large settlements in one part of the economy are copied across other sectors. Companies set prices not so much in response to changes in supply and demand, as in response to what is happening to their unit costs. They try to keep a fairly constant mark-up, and the growth of multinationals, and of monopolies and cartels among producers, has made it much easier for them to get away with this. Money wages are highly inflexible downwards, say Keynesians, and prices are not much better.

The most common causes of inflation are thus external shocks to the price structure — such as the rise in the world oil price in the early 1970s, or the increase in trade-union militancy at the end of the 1960s. If the level of demand falls, that may even initially contribute to inflation: it will raise companies' costs, because they will be able to sell fewer goods while carrying the same overheads. If companies do indeed aim for a fairly steady mark-up, they may even raise their prices rather than lowering them.

Monetarists, in other words, emphasize the importance of the market, and of shifts in supply and demand, in setting prices. Keynesians tend to emphasize the imperfections of the market in the complicated economy of the modern world, and think that supply or demand may adjust more freely than prices.

The point comes out more clearly when one looks at the Keynesian view of the monetarist cure for inflation. Keynesians usually argue that the cure for inflation lies in incomes policy – or more broadly, in reforming the structure of collective bargaining. The monetarist cure for inflation, they argue, is simply a recipe for a slump. While an expansion of monetary growth may make faster inflation possible, the main effect of slower monetary growth will be on output. Workers will not accept a cut in their living standards, and companies will not reduce prices. The rate of unemployment will rise, and inflation will persist. Eventually, many Keynesians concede, the familiar technique of scaring workers into accepting lower pay increases may work. But it may involve a much higher rate of unemployment than the government's nerve will stand and than is necessary.

It may also involve higher interest rates than politicians are prepared to tolerate. In the Keynesian heyday, the main purpose of monetary policy was to keep interest rates as low as possible. But high interest rates are an inevitable part of the first stages of a monetary policy which is attempting to bring down the rate of inflation. Interest rates are the mechanism – they are the way in which the government attracts savings to pay for its borrowing, and the way in which companies are deterred from borrowing from the banks. They also help to choke off demand in a variety of ways by hitting stocks, fixed investment, and such consumer spending as is financed by borrowing.

When monetarism first came back into academic fashion, in the late 1960s and early 1970s, it was widely thought that the political fear of high unemployment would be the main threat to effective monetary policy. In fact, in many countries the main threat turned out to come from the political fear of high interest rates.

Keynesians do not just argue that relying on monetary policy to cure inflation may cause more damage than it cures. They do not share the faith of the monetarists that the economy is self-stabilizing. It is for this reason that the whole development of post-war demand management – the attempt to adjust the

10

level of demand by deliberate acts of government policy — has been under the guidance of Keynesian economists. The idea that the government can and should take responsibility for the level of demand, and consequently for the rate of unemployment, is essentially a reflection of the influence of Keynes.

Keynesians are also far from convinced that the government can accurately control the money supply. Before I explain their doubts, it might help to look at what the government is trying to control and at how it is trying to do it.

Money may be moved in a number of ways. Very few people today would argue that the right measure is simply the notes which the Bank of England prints and the coins which it mints. The reason is that what most people use as money does not stop at the currency in circulation. Many people are as willing to pay the bill at the supermarket check-out with a cheque as with cash. Indeed most transactions which take place in the economy are not paid for in cash (whatever your window-cleaner thinks) but by transferring claims on the banks. That mainly consists of writing cheques. So the narrowest measure of the money supply in common use (Ml) is composed of notes and coins in circulation, plus sight deposits (mainly current accounts) held by the UK private sector.*

That is not, however, the thing which the Chancellor of the Exchequer is talking about when he mentions the money supply. The targets for growth are set in terms of 'sterling M3'. That includes all sterling deposits held by UK residents in both the public and private sectors: in other words, it includes deposit accounts, and sterling certificates of deposit.

Many people point out that it is illogical to include bank deposit accounts in sterling M3 but to exclude building society accounts. The result of this arbitrary distinction is that each time banks offer better interest rates than the building societies, encouraging people to switch their money around, the money supply appears to be rising. Wily monetarists hedge their bets by arguing that one ought to look at a wide range of monetary indicators to know what monetary conditions are doing.

But monetary policy involves attempting to control what the money supply is doing, as well as using it as an indicator.* The two main components of sterling M3 are net purchases of public sector debt by the banks, and sterling bank lending. Take these one by one. When the public sector borrows, it can raise cash from two main sources. First, it can tap savings. It may do this by selling gilt-edged securities (Treasury 9% 1994, for instance) to a pension fund or a life assurance company, or by selling premium bonds to old ladies. If it does that − if it borrows real savings − it is generally held not to be increasing the supply of money.* But if the government borrows by selling government debt to the banks, it is usually seen as increasing the money supply. The reason is that the gilt-edged securities increase the assets on the bank's balance sheet. Broadly speaking, an increase in assets allows a bank to increase its liabilities. So a bank can accept extra deposits and lend more money. Thus the money supply increases.*

Sterling bank lending affects the money supply in much the same way. If a bank makes a new loan, it acquires a new asset on its own balance sheet. But the borrower will put the money into a bank so it becomes a new deposit − and so, again, the money supply increases.

So government monetary policy tries to reduce the amount the public sector borrows to a level which is more in line with the savings which the economy generates each year. And it tries to reduce bank borrowing by the rest of the private sector. Its central aim is to limit the sum of these two parts of monetary growth to match the growth in the volume of production.

There are, of course, a number of problems. For some time, a number of economists − most vocally, Lord Kaldor − have been arguing that there is very little evidence in the past decade to support the contention that there is a stable link between the amount the public sector borrows and the behaviour of the money supply. Worse for monetarism, it increasingly looks as though it is very difficult for the government to control bank lending to the private sector. Companies simply do not respond very quickly to high interest rates. Indeed the monetarists' critics would claim that the rate of growth of the money supply was just as likely to be determined by the demand for money as by the direct attempts of the government to influence the supply. It may be that the rate at which prices rise determines the growth of the money supply, rather than the opposite. Companies borrow from the banks because they need working capital; and their demand for working capital is more likely to be influenced by the size of their wages bill than by the level of interest rates. If wages are rising rapidly, then even high interest rates will not prevent bank borrowing from rising, at least in the short term.

This may seem a long way from the simple problem of curing inflation: the problem which attracted Margaret Thatcher and the Conservatives to monetarism. The sad truth seems to be that controlling the growth of the money supply, in the short or medium term, is technically more difficult than the early monetarists believed. Controlling it without large fluctuations in interest rates is more difficult still. But if monetary policy does not hold out the hope of curing inflation, what does?

An essential part of the Keynesian answer usually would be incomes policy. But it is also very difficult to be optimistic about incomes policy. It is a block around which the UK has marched many times in the last couple of decades. There was the pay pause of 1961, followed a year later by the establishment of the National Incomes Commission and the announcement of a $2\frac{1}{2}\%$ pay 'norm'. Then in 1964, the new Labour Government abolished the National Incomes Commission. The following year, it set up the the National Board for Prices and Incomes to administer a 3 to $3\frac{1}{2}\%$ norm. Between then and 1970, Labour governments experimented alternately with voluntary controls and a statutory freeze. By November 1972, Edward Heath's Conservative government had re-introduced a freeze on pay and prices. Having abolished the Prices and Incomes Board, the Conservatives in 1972 set up a Pay Board to administer their incomes policy. Edwards Heath's policy struggled on into 1974. By the time the incoming Labour government wound up the Pay Board, it was approving settlements of over 9%. The Labour government survived until mid 1975 without an incomes policy. Its policy of voluntary restraint lasted longer and was probably more effective than any previous efforts: but by the time the Conservatives won the 1979 election, Labour's policy had lost the support of the trade unions and was patently having no impact on pay bargaining. Just to complete the picture, the Conservative government lived with unfettered collective bargaining for just over a year, and then announced a 6% limit

13

on the cash available to pay for central and local government pay awards.

So all governments over the past twenty years, with the arguable exception of the present Conservative one, have found that they could not cope without an incomes policy. But all incomes policies in the past have become progressively less effective at restraining pay.

To end this chapter, I want to look at two points. First, why is it that incomes policies have never lasted? And second, is there any economic rationale behind incomes policies which makes them worth persevering with?

Incomes policies, as even the sketchy account in this chapter suggests, tend to follow a similar pattern. The first stage is usually a complete freeze. The public tends to regard this as fairest, because it is the most easily understood and the most readily observed form of policy. But a freeze cannot endure for long. Even if it is combined with a price freeze, the prices of imports change. People change jobs: people enter and leave the workforce. Even if the overall level of pay is stable, wages for individual jobs need to change to reflect the changing supply of, and demand for, that kind of labour. So a freeze is a breathing-space, not a policy.

Most policies revolve around a target number of some sort. If pay is not frozen, then it is likely to rise. If it is to be allowed to rise, people want to know by how much. Sooner or later, the government produces the figure for the average rise in wages it thinks the economy can stand. But no shop steward wants to be seen negotiating for less than the average for his union members. So the average becomes a floor — and unless the government has played a game of double bluff, pay inevitably rises by more than the number the government first thought of.

By how much more depends partly on how the policy is enforced. A policy with the vigorous backing of the trade unions seems to be more likely to last than one without — which is unfortunate for Conservative governments which do not have good relations with the unions. A policy with simple rules is easier to enforce than a complicated one.

But a policy with simple rules makes fewer allowances for anomalies and for the complications of the pay market. What

14

happens, for instance, if a company wants to make a massive improvement in the pension scheme it runs for its workers while an incomes policy is in force? Should that be counted as far-sighted altruism, or an attempt to bend the rules? What happens if Mr Bloggs, the Assistant Deputy Widget Supervisor on £8000 a year is made Assistant Deputy Widget Supervisor With Special Responsibility for Information Control on £8500 a year? Is that legitimate re-grading, or a way of giving Mr Bloggs an illegal rise? How should the policy deal with workers on piece-rates, or with overtime payments? How should it deal with the self-employed, or with the recipients of dividend income? How should it deal with workers who genuinely increase their productivity — and how does anyone know that a real productivity increase has taken place? Should it make special exceptions for very low-paid workers, and if so, what happens when their differential with the fairly low-paid is eroded? It is no wonder, confronted with questions like these, that the survival rate of incomes policy has not been wildly impressive.

Nor is it any wonder that incomes policies which really bite leave behind them a wake of anomalies: relative pay rates out of line with past tradition, overtime rates out of line with basic pay, fringe benefits out of line with salaries and so on. That might not matter if there were incontrovertible evidence that incomes policy restrained the rate of growth of money wages. It might be worth creating some anomalies in the pay pattern: after all, there are plenty already. The trouble is that there is some evidence now to suggest that incomes policy may only postpone, not prevent, a rise in pay. Workers, so the argument runs, want to see their real incomes rise by a certain amount from year to year. They may be persuaded to sacrifice an improvement in living standards for a while when an incomes policy is in force, but once the policy is removed, they will try to make up for all the ground they have lost. At the end of the day, pay will have risen by just as much as if there had never been any incomes policy at all.

So why do governments continue to introduce pay policies? There is usually, of course, an element of desperation: pay rises get out of hand, an election starts to loom alarmingly close, and so on. But incomes policy is also, in a sense, an employment policy. For the only alternative which Keynesians can offer to slow the growth of money wages is to reduce the pressure of demand in the economy. Given their view of the weak links between what happens to pay and the general state of the job market, Keynesians tend to accept that such a policy involves a very large rise in unemployment and loss of output in order to achieve a small decline in the pace of inflation. Direct controls on wages are thus the only way of minimizing the rise in unemployment associates with a reduction in the rate of inflation. As I said earlier in this chapter, monetarists might logically argue for incomes policy too, as a way of altering expectations about inflation; but monetarists are apt to take a more sanguine view of the influence of unemployment on pay.

But if workers do indeed have a target rise in their living standards in their minds, and pursue it come hell or high water, then that is not a point scored by monetarists against Keynesians. It simply suggests that the method of fixing wages cannot be reconciled with the economic facts of life. For the economy cannot necessarily continue, year after year, to deliver the pay awards people think they deserve. If it is forced to do so, the result will be rising unemployment. The reason why every government, sooner or later, falls back on incomes policy may be that it is the only way so far discovered of altering the way wages are fixed. Without a reform of the system of pay bargaining, the economics profession may have to admit that it simply does not have a politically workable cure for inflation to offer.

2 Public expenditure: how should it be controlled?

'Public expenditure is at the heart of Britain's economic difficulties.'*

Thus the opening sentence of the first White Paper published by the Conservative government on its future spending plans (Cmnd 7746, November 1979[1]). The government's second White Paper (Cmnd 7841) opened with an equally forthright statement: 'The government intend to reduce public expenditure progressively in volume terms over the next four years'.*

The Conservative government, under Margaret Thatcher, has put more emphasis on the control of public expenditure than its predecessors, because of the importance it attaches to the control of the money supply, and because of its belief that government borrowing is a major component of monetary growth. This point is explained in chapter 1. The government has also been worried by the burden on the taxpayer, who finances the bulk of public spending. This point is developed in the next chapter (3). This chapter looks at two other aspects of the debate. First, it reviews the way public spending is planned – for the method has been undergoing dramatic changes. Second, it looks at the arguments which surround the opening controversial sentence from the first Conservative White Paper; and it raises the issue posed in the second sentence quoted: if public spending is indeed to be reduced, how best can that be done?

[1] Copies of White Papers are available from HMSO in London.

The story of the planning of public expenditure is the tale of the efforts of successive governments to get to grips with three serious dilemmas. First, there is the problem of choosing a time-horizon. Some decisions have to be taken a long way in advance. A decision today to build a motorway will involve expenditure ten years hence. But to try to plan all spending ten years hence is to invite failure. Second, there is the problem of dealing with inflation. Planning in the past, as this chapter shows, has been in terms of volume — of numbers of teachers, tons of cement, miles of road for example. Plans drawn up that way are very hard to use as instruments of control when prices are changing rapidly. But plans cast entirely in terms of today's money may lead people to think too much about the implications for government borrowing, and not enough about the cost in terms of national resources.

Third and most important is the problem of coping with un-expected fluctuations, be they in prices, in needs or in available resources. If there is a public sector pay explosion, or a sudden surge in unemployment, or a rise in the price of oil, how should the government react? Ought it to have some 'soft' plans which can be cut easily? And how can it best relate plans to an effective system of control? In trying to solve these dilemmas, govern-ments have moved round in a circle in the past twenty years: from a Gladstonian preoccupation with the year immediately ahead, to an attempt at long-term planning, and back to a year-by-year concern with cash totals.

The way in which governments plan public spending has changed quite substantially over the recent past. It was only in the late 1950s that it began to be accepted that spending plans needed to run for more than the years immediately ahead. Up to then, only a few items, such as defence, had been systematically planned ahead. Otherwise, the government of the day set out its spending plans very much as it would have done under Glad-stone, in Parliamentary estimates and — when the estimates were exceeded as the financial year wore on — supplementary estimates.

The first major change came in the wake of a committee set up under Lord Plowden in 1959. When the committee reported in 1961, it took as its test the principle that 'decisions involving substantial future expenditure should always be taken in the light of surveys of public expenditure as a whole, over a number of years and in relation to the prospective resources'.

From 1961 onwards, there began the convention of making an annual survey of public expenditure covering a period of five years, rolled forward one year at a time. I will come back to this exercise in a moment, as it still forms the basis of public expenditure projection today. It had one peculiar characteristic: right up to and including the Public Expenditure White Paper of 1981, the five year survey was carried out in terms of volume. That inevitably created a fundamental weakness in the system as inflation gathered pace.

Indeed, the problem of coping with the impact of inflation on public spending has been central to the whole debate on public expenditure control for over a decade. The crux of the difficulty is how the public sector should react if the price of a pencil, or the pay of a nurse, rises relative to other prices and wages in the economy. Ought the volume of public spending be cut? Or should the taxpayers have to pay more for the same quality of service? The question mattered particularly as public spending plans began to be used for public spending control.

In the 1969 White Paper, the first of the annual series of public spending White Papers, there was a first attempt to take some account of inflation in planning public spending, through the invention of a concept called the Relative Price Effect (RPE). The RPE is a shorthand way of expressing the fact that costs and prices in the public sector tend to rise at a different pace from prices in the economy as a whole. Usually, because the public sector is more labour intensive and because it is much harder to get increases in productivity, public sector costs rise faster than those in the private sector. Then the RPE is said to be positive.*

The RPE is a way of setting out the fact that even if public expenditure does not grow in volume terms, the demands it makes on the economy may rise over time. It is the point I was making above. Even if the total number of local authority manual workers does not increase, if their pay rises faster than private sector pay, it will cost a bigger proportion of output to employ them.

Through the 1960s and the early 1970s, public expenditure was very much thought of as part of the government's weaponry of demand management. This was one reason for the concentration on planning in volume terms. The annual planning exercise was just that: a planning operation, with what in retrospect looks an amazingly sketchy attempt to match plans to what actually happened.

The result was an almost inexorable tendency for public expenditure to creep upwards. In five of the six White Papers published between 1971 and 1976, public expenditure plans were revised upwards. The most dramatic increase was in 1975. In December 1976, the House of Commons Expenditure Committee published a report on the financing of public expenditure in which it concluded 'Even allowing for unannounced policy changes, the Treasury's present methods of controlling public expenditure are inadequate, in the sense that money can be spent on a scale which was not contemplated when the relevant policies were decided upon'. The Committee pointed out that public expenditure in 1974–5, at 1974–5 prices, was about £5.8 billions more than had been planned in the White Paper of November 1971. The Treasury had said in evidence that about £1.8 billions of this was the result of announced policy changes. But nearly 70% of the increase, the Committee pointed out, was not the result of announced policy changes. That amounted to 5% of the UK's gross domestic product.

Nearly half of the excess had been the result of unforeseen increases in the prices paid by the public sector, relative to those paid by the private sector. Easily the most important reason was the huge rise in land and construction costs which took place between 1970–1 and 1974–5.

These events were largely responsible for the subsequent development of cash limits. They were first applied to some central and local government building programmes in 1974–5 and 1975–6. In 1976, the government extended them to cover roughly 40% of all central government expenditure, as well as local government capital spending, the rate support grant to local authorities, and the borrowing needs of the nationalized industries.

Cash limits are used in different ways in different parts of the public sector. On the spending of the central government, they simply mean that there is a limit to the amount of cash which can be spent in each defined block of expenditure. They do not cover the whole of central government spending. There are quite large areas which are taken to be 'demand determined' — such as unemployment benefit, or grants to industry. But in those areas which are covered, cash limits are a direct restriction on the amount of money which can be spent.

The same is true of local government capital spending — the investment programmes of local authorities. The central government says precisely how much local authorities can spend on housing programmes, road programmes, and so on. But the current spending of local authorities — expenditure on their pay bills, and on day-to-day purchases of goods and services — and the spending of the nationalized industries have to be treated in a different way.

In the case of local government, each autumn the cabinet decides on a cash limit on the Rate Support Grant. That constrains, in terms of hard cash, the amount which central government is prepared to pay to supplement the authorities' income from rates and from charges. As the Rate Support Grant makes up almost two-thirds of local authorities' revenues, that is quite an effective control over their total current spending. But of course, local authorities determined to spend more can always consider putting up the rates.

With nationalized industries, the cash limit is not the same sort of concept. It is a constraint on the industries' ability to borrow funds from sources other than the government — and indeed, the term 'cash limit' has generally been replaced by 'External Financing Limit' (EFL). The limit does not directly affect the wages that nationalized industries can afford to pay, nor the rate at which their other costs rise. For if the government sets an EFL on, say, the Post Office which assumes that pay will only rise by 6% and instead the Post Office allows its pay bill to rise by 10%, there are other ways in which the Post Office can raise money. It can cut its investment programme; it can put up the price of stamps, secure in the knowledge that it has a virtual monopoly of mail delivery; or it can cut its running costs by reducing the service it offers customers — by cutting collections or second deliveries, for instance.

Pay accounts for just over half of all central government spending. So setting cash limits forces a government to take a view about the likely rise in pay in the coming year. From there it is a very small step to something close to a public sector pay policy: from saying 'We think pay will rise by 6% next year and that is what our cash limits are designed to finance' to saying 'We think pay ought to rise by no more than 6% next year and if it goes up by more, then the numbers of public sector employees − or some other bit of public spending − will have to be cut to foot the bill'.

Cash limits essentially represented an attempt to graft on a new system of control to the system of planning public spending which grew up in the late 1960s and 1970s. Over the years to 1981, it gradually became clear that this half-way house was not good enough. The upshot has been a decision to abandon planning in terms of volume for planning in terms of cash. But before looking at the new system, it might be useful to see how the old one operated.

The cycle began − and still begins − in the spring. Under the whole system, the first stage used to be for individual government departments to convert the previous year's White Paper into a new set of 'survey prices'. These were the prices used for all the arithmetic of the main planning exercise, and they were the prices ruling in the autumn before the whole exercise began. They were chosen because they were the most recent known when public spending plans began to be made; but by the time the White Paper came to be published, they were anything up to eighteen months old. The White Paper of March 1981 − the last one to use survey prices − was in terms of 1980 survey prices, which were the prices of autumn 1979.

Government departments would then work out what the policies they were currently implementing would cost, with any announced policies added on, and translate the lot into the prices of the previous autumn. The plans would then be rolled forward one year: in spring 1980, departments were sketching out how much they thought they might be spending in 1983−4.

Together with these baseline projections, government departments were also supposed to make additional bids − claims for spending on the new programmes they would like to have — and to set out what they would cut if they had to. In late March, the Treasury began to talk about these figures with individual spending departments, trying to spot a bit of padding here and to push for a more realistic set of possible cuts there.

These initial discussions and negotiations used to, indeed still do, take place under the supervision of the Public Expenditure Survey Committee (PESC). This is a large committee on which sit the Principal Finance Officers of all the spending departments. It is chaired by a Treasury Deputy Secretary. In late May, or thereabouts, the PESC takes the figures which have emerged from the Treasury's talks and turns them into a report to ministers illustrating what would happen to public expenditure if the previous White Paper projections continue to be applied. This then goes to the ministers. In late June or early July, there is the first round of cabinet discussions. You often know that it is happening because the newspapers are suddenly full of awful stories about the draconian spending cuts which are on the way. These tend to be leaked by a disconcerted minister of a spending department, anxious to whip up a lobby to help him fight off the impending axe.

When ministers come back from their summer holidays, the exercise gathers pace. In early autumn, the Treasury carries out an economic forecast. One version of this forecast is produced in terms of current prices, and it includes a figure for planned public expenditure. On this, the Chancellor bases his calculation about the possible size of the next year's borrowing requirement. He can then make a judgement about whether he thinks public spending is likely to be too high or too low for the next year.

Under the old method of planning public spending, the size of the change that the Chancellor might want to make then had to be translated back into survey prices — 'funny money', as critics of this elaborate system labelled it. The reason was that any cuts (or in rare years, increases) had to be shared out department by department; and the figure for total public spending in terms of hard cash could not be broken that way. The picture of public spending had been built up in survey price (or volume) terms and could only be dissected that way.

Now on upshot of this elaborate dance between one price system and another was monumental confusion. If it muddles you, imagine what it did to the average cabinet minister. The Chancellor would find himself talking to his colleagues in terms of two different kinds of prices — current prices for the next year's borrowing requirement, and survey prices for departmental spending bids.

There was another problem. For at this stage, the cabinet had to decide what it thought the rate of inflation in the coming financial year was likely to be, in order to set cash limits. It is, after all, the actual cost of public expenditure which affects the amount which the public sector is likely to borrow in the year ahead — the public sector borrowing requirement — and that is the number which the government regards as important to its control over the growth of the money supply.

In fixing cash limits for the year ahead under the old system, the government was trying to do two things at the same time. It was trying to make sure that it knew what its planned programmes would cost in actual money in the coming financial year; and it was sometimes also trying to constrain the rise in public sector costs. If the cash limit for the coming year was set below what the rise in public sector costs was really likely to turn out to be, then the inevitable result would be a further cut in the *volume* of public spending.

This meant that ministers had to fight the same battle twice over. First there would be an argument about what the volume of public spending ought to be in the coming year. Then there would be a second argument about cash limits, which might end up deliberately being set so low that it became a virtual certainty that the volume plans set in the first debate would be unattainable.

The decisions taken by the cabinet in the autumn are then translated into the public expenditure White Paper. It used to be published around the turn of the year, but the current Conservative government has sensibly decided to produce it at the same time as the Budget. Until it did so, Britain was virtually alone among industrial countries in separating the budget tax-raising exercise completely from public expenditure planning.

The Public Expenditure White Paper itself is traditionally a document of almost unintelligible complexity. The amount of information which it discloses rises and falls as governments move in and out of economic crises. Thus it sometimes (but not always) offers a long-term view of the economy against which the spending decisions are supposed to have been taken. It rarely tries to guess at the one thing we would all like to know: the implications for taxation which the decisions imply.

Up to and including the White Paper of March 1981, there was a multiplicity of totals for public spending on offer. You could choose from among:

1 Expenditure on programmes: this simply added up the spending plans of central government, local government and a motley collection of public corporations ranging from the Bank of England the BBC to the Crown Agents and the National Ports Council.
2 Total public expenditure before shortfall and special sales of assets: this was the planning total, plus the contingency reserve — the safety margin built into White Papers to finance unforeseen events and changes of policy, plus debt interest. Debt interest is always put in separately because there is no way that it can be planned ahead.
3 Planning total: this was the sum of the spending on programmes, the contingency reserve and net borrowing overseas and in the capital market by nationalized industries. It excluded debt interest.
4 Planning total after shortfall: this took in everything in the planning total, but reduced it by deducting a 'general allowance for shortfall'. This was intended to take account of the fact that cash limits have tended to encourage underspending. Programme managers wisely aim to spend a little less than their limits allow, to give themselves a margin of safety. This total was often the smallest in the White Paper, and the one on which governments concentrated attention.
5 Public expenditure in cost terms: this usually appeared at the back of the White Paper. Unlike all the other totals, it added on (or deducted) an allowance for the relative price effect. It added to the total cost of programmes the contingency reserve and the cost of debt interest.

This last total — public expenditure in cost terms — is the most important. It allows a comparison of the expected growth in the cost of public spending programmes with the expected growth of the economy as a whole. In other words it is the total from which it is possible to calculate the demands made by the public sector on total national resources. This is, after all, the relationship which ultimately is of most concern to the government and to the taxpayer. Even with public expenditure planned in terms of current prices, it therefore remains essential to be able to measure it in cost terms too.

Now if this description has dodged uneasily between the past and present tense, it is because in March 1981 the government announced that it intended to abandon the practice of planning public spending in volume terms, and switch to using cash. It is a radical decision, which ought to make public spending plans far more understandable to the ordinary person than the old order did. But if it comes to that, almost anything would be easier to understand than the old system.

Under the new regime, there will be no need for spending departments to update their policies to take account of inflation since the previous White Paper. They will simply have to say how much money their policies are currently costing and what they expect the policies to cost, in actual money, in the financial year ahead. This means, of course, that from early on in the exercise the government will need to have a guess at the rate of inflation for the year ahead. When the exercise begins in the spring, the guess will have to stretch over two years to the end of the next financial year. By the autumn, the guess will have to become quite firm.

That will not be easy: although it will make it possible for everyone to talk about next year's spending in terms of what next year's prices are really likely to be. It will also impose a tougher constraint on spending departments. For in spite of cash limits, there were still many times under the old system when cash did not really act as a constraint. Take road-building for example. If the Department of the Environment is building a new motorway, it probably negotiates contracts between summer and Christmas for work in the following financial year. By the time cash limits for that year are set, the cost of the contract will have become 'current prices'. That gives no incentive to say to construction firms 'We can't afford that increase'.

The main reason why there has been so much pressure to find a better way to control public spending is that governments have become more worried about the rate at which it has grown.* Public spending has to be paid for, either from taxation or from government borrowing. In the 1970s, there were some signs that the state might be approaching the limit of the amount of tax which people were prepared to pay under the present system. It is true that Britain is not a particularly heavily taxed country by European standards. If one adds together personal taxation and social security payments in the UK and looks at them as a proportion of gross domestic product (GDP), the ratio is not outstandingly high. Indeed in 1977, before Margaret Thatcher took office, the UK already came below France and West Germany.

But over the past twenty years, the number of taxpayers in the economy has increased enormously to a point where almost every person in a full-time job pays income tax. This is in part simply a reflection of our greater affluence: poor taxpayers earn as much, adjusted for inflation, as better-off people did two decades ago. But as the tax net has been stretched wider, so it appears that evasion may have increased. It looks as though workers may try to win back money they lose to the Inland Revenue in higher tax payments by demanding higher money wages. In other words, rising taxation may possibly be a contributory factor in pay demands. The Labour government in the mid-1970s tried to counteract this by talking about the 'social wage': the value of goods and services which individuals received free or subsidized from the state. But it looks as though workers do not normally think of the 'social wage' as part of their pay.

Apart from resistance to increases in the tax burden, there has been another reason why governments have become worried about allowing public spending to rise. The new interest in monetarism in the 1970s drew attention to the amount the government borrowed. If the government borrows short-term, monetarists argue, it risks expanding the money supply and

27

fuelling inflation. If it borrows long-term, it pre-empts finance which industry needs.

So the Conservative government took office in 1979 determined to reduce the total of public spending. The Conservatives made it sound as though Labour had allowed public spending to rip. In fact, the volume of public expenditure was lower in 1978−9, and indeed in 1979−80, than it had been when Harold Wilson's government took office. And in two of the Labour government's five years, public spending fell very sharply indeed. In 1977−8, it was actually lower in volume terms than the level to which the Conservative government hoped to reduce it by 1983−4.

Thanks to the Labour government's cuts, the total cost of public expenditure programmes in volume terms in 1980−1 was actually below the cost in 1974−5. Indeed the cost of programmes − of education, social security, the health service, and so on − all added together now appears to have peaked in 1975−6. The cost of debt interest on the other hand has risen sharply. The total in 1980−1 was well over double the 1975−6 amount.

So the Labour government did actually manage to reduce the volume of public expenditure quite dramatically. But when one looks at what has happened to the composition of public expenditure, it becomes clear that this was achieved in a way which will make it very hard to find other large cuts in future.

The volume of public spending by central government (excluding lending to nationalized industries) has risen, and spending by local authorities has dropped in almost every year since 1974−5. The March 1981 Public Expenditure White Paper accepted that there would be a further rise in the volume of central government spending and fall in that of local authorities in 1981−2. One of the main reasons for this pattern has been the sharp decline in capital spending, relative to current. The White Paper of March 1980 (Cmnd 7841) planned for total capital spending of £7781 million. In 1974−5, the first year covered by that White Paper, capital spending ran at £15,050 million. In other words, the total was expected to be about half that of earlier years.

Current expenditure on the other hand has risen persistently.

The March 1981 White Paper (Cmnd 8175) actually planned for a further increase between 1980—1 and 1981—2. Total current spending in volume terms in 1981—2 was planned to be nearly 10% higher than it had been in 1975—6. The overwhelming reason for this rise was not — as you might perhaps imagine — an increase in the public sector wage and salary bill. That has gone up but by nothing like as much as one single category: current grants to persons. That rose between 1975—6 and 1980—1 by just over 30%. Between 1980—1 and 1981—2, the March 1981 White Paper projected a further rise of 6.6%. That brought this particular category to 30% of total public spending. Almost all of this category consists of social security payments.

There have been some special reasons for this increase. For instance, the cost of child benefit rose sharply when the Labour government abolished the child tax allowance. But most of the increase has come from two sources: from retirement pensions, for which the bill has risen as the number of elderly people has increased, and from unemployment benefit and associated payments.

And with this, we come to the heart of the dilemma which confronted the Conservative government in its anxiety to reduce total public expenditure by 1983—4. For it found that cuts had to be concentrated at the hard core of public spending: on the big programmes of defence (a tenth of the total), education and health (each a seventh), or social security, on which more than £1 in every £4 of public expenditure now goes. But cutting social security is an idea which many people find almost impossible to accept, particularly in the depths of a profound recession.

In the main the other options have already been tried. Capital expenditure has been pared down to a point where in 1980—1 it was actually less than the public sector borrowing requirement. In other words, the government was borrowing to pay its pay bill and social security obligations: not to finance investment.

In its first eighteen months in office — a period when the volume of public spending continued to rise, in spite of all the talk of 'massive Tory cuts' — the Conservative government tried to cut spending mainly in ways which passed the burden on to the private sector. For instance, it increased council house rents. More dramatically, it pushed the nationalized industries into raising their prices in an effort to reduce the amount of money they borrowed from the public purse. But in spite of its efforts, lending by the central government to the nationalized industries actually increased between 1980—1 and 1981—2.

Leaving aside the question of cutting the social security bill, the only long-term way of reducing public spending probably will be to reduce the size of the public sector. There are undoubtedly many services which the public sector provides which could be provided by the private sector. For instance, before the council house was thought of, rented accommodation was provided entirely by the private sector; before the public library came into being, Boots performed the service (for a fee) all over the country; and there are in existence in Britain today private hospitals, private refuse collection services, private schools and even a private university to show what might be done by a government absolutely determined to reduce the size of the public sector.

The option is most obvious in the case of the nationalized industries. The 1979 Conservative government was more restrained than some of its Tory predecessors about selling back to the private sector, industries taken into the public sector by a Labour government. But British Aerospace has been denationalized, and the British National Oil Corporation is expected to be sold to private shareholders. However, these two industries are rather special cases: both are highly profitable. A much more difficult question is, say, what to do about British Rail. The government could save itself a lot of money if it could persuade ICI to take over British Rail. ICI might reduce the loss that British Rail now makes by running the system more efficiently; the railways are still heavily overmanned. But the other options would be to raise fares still further; or to close down all those parts of the rail network which are currently highly subsidized and which carry a handful of passengers at vast expense to distant corners of the Celtic fringe.*

With the main services which the government provides — particularly with education and health — the choice eventually may be between finding a way of charging for them, or drastically reducing the scale of the service.* Up to now, governments have chosen to cut services: national museums have reduced their hours rather than charge an entrance fee, libraries close early rather than charge for membership. The usual argument is that the sheer cost of collecting the money would mop up most of the revenue; and that people who ought to be encouraged to use public services would be discouraged. Neither point is very convincing. Without any system of charging, it is impossible to gauge how much the public really wants any particular public service: the fuss about cuts often comes from public sector unions rather than the consuming public.*

It may in fact be the case that the growth of public spending on education and health has largely reflected rising public demand for these services, as incomes increase. Demand for private education and health has shown a tendency to increase very rapidly. If that is indeed true, then the question is whether people would rather pay through taxation or from their own pockets. As the axe begins to fall, the answer may become clearer.

3 Taxation: why do we pay it?

Why do we pay tax? The short answer is 'to finance the spending of the state'. State spending is not new; after all, the Domesday Book was intended to increase tax yield by giving a clearer idea of how rich medieval England was. But as public expenditure has soared in the post-war years, so the burden of taxation has also increased enormously.

Broadly speaking, there are three bases on which people can be taxed. You can tax their wealth. This is the oldest kind of tax: wealth, at least in the form of land and houses, is hard to hide. We have two main taxes on wealth: local authority rates (which people do not think of as a wealth tax, but which tends to operate like one) and Capital Transfer Tax, levied when wealth changes hands. Perhaps one could argue that Vehicle Excise Duty was a sort of wealth tax too. But unlike most other European countries, we do not have a proper wealth tax, though it is the Labour party's long-running favourite tax reform.

Then you can tax spending. We raise a smaller proportion of total tax revenue through indirect taxes than most other countries do, although the gap has diminished since Value Added Tax (VAT) replaced purchase tax. VAT apart, there is a whole gamut of 'specific duties', flat rate imposts levied by Customs and Excise (not the Inland Revenue). Far and away the most important fall on tobacco, alcoholic drink, and petrol. Taken together, these taxes on spending yield about as much as income tax.*

And finally, you can tax income. Income tax produces more

money by far than any other single tax — roughly twice as much as VAT. But it is not the only way we tax income. Although the government still sticks to the fiction that national insurance contributions are not a tax, they have exactly the same effect as one. Moreover, as employers' national insurance contributions fall directly on to their pay bills, they are, at least partly, effectively paid by employees. By way of comparison, take the figures for 1980–1. National insurance contributions (collected by the Department of Health and Social Security) totalled about £17.5 billion, and the national insurance surcharge (collected by the Inland Revenue) yielded a further £3.5 billion. That is very nearly as much as the total yield from income tax.

The way in which governments use these three options depends to a large extent on how they want to see income and wealth distributed among the population. The balance of government expenditure and taxation is, of course, one of the instruments which governments use to try to expand or reduce the rate of activity in the economy. But the particular shape of the tax structure is determined very much by the prevailing attitude to distribution. This varies depending on which political party is in power. The Conservative party tends to treat the rich more kindly than the Labour party, and not surprisingly, one of the first acts of Margaret Thatcher's government was to reduce the very high rates of income tax on large salaries. But the variation is not as great as you might think when listening to politicians. It is now generally accepted that the rich should pay a larger proportion of their income in tax than the poor. And it is widely agreed that one of the aims of taxation ought to be to narrow the gap between the incomes and the wealth of the rich and of the poor.*

It is easier to see how taxing income and wealth can narrow this gap than it is to see how taxing expenditure can affect it. The reason is that taxes on income and on wealth can fairly easily be made 'progressive' — taking a larger percentage from the wealthy than from the poor. Taxes on spending seem, at first sight, to be inevitably proportional: taking the same percentage from rich and from poor. But whether they are or not depends on what they fall upon. If every household spends the same fraction of its income on newspapers, then an indirect tax on newspapers will indeed be proportional. But there are very few goods or services of which that is true in reality. Most indirect taxes are likely to be regressive — taking proportionately more from the poor than the rich — simply because the poor spend more of their total incomes than the rich. Some indirect taxes are highly regressive — the poor spend much more of their incomes on cigarettes than the better-off, who actually tend to smoke less. A few — duty on alcohol for instance — are actually progressive in their effect.

Most people firmly believe that Britain is one of the most over-taxed countries in the world. Margaret Thatcher arguably won an election on that myth. For it is a myth. What the figures show is that we come in the middle range of industrial countries, and always have done. We are nowhere near as highly taxed as the Swedes or the Norwegians. But neither do we get away as lightly as the Americans or the Japanese. Add together all taxes and social security contributions, measure them against gross national product (GNP), and in 1978 Britain emerged seventh in the league table of industrial countries. We paid less tax, relative to the total size of our economy, than Sweden, Norway, Belgium, the Netherlands; and less than France and West Germany too.*

That was before Margaret Thatcher set out to cut taxes. It is a policy in which she failed, at least in her first two years in office. As Nigel Lawson, the Financial Secretary, admitted in January 1981, the burden of taxation has continued to rise.

The figures were as follows. In 1973—4, the last year of Edward Heath's government, taxes including local authority rates and national insurance contributions were equivalent to 38.5% of GNP at factor cost. By the last year of the Labour government, 1978—9, that had risen to 40%. In Margaret Thatcher's first year in office, the proportion rose to 42.5%. In 1980—1, it rose further, perhaps to 45%.

Some figures show how the rise in the tax burden has affected individual families. In 1978—9, a married couple with two children and with only the husband at work, paid average male earnings, would have found themselves paying 24% of their income in income tax and employees' national insurance contributions, and about $10\frac{1}{2}\%$ in indirect taxes. The following year, the couple would have paid a bit less, 23.7%, of their income in direct tax and contributions, but 12.4% in indirect taxes. That reflects the big jump in VAT in the first Conservative budget. In 1980−1, the typical couple paid 24.8% of their income in income tax and national insurance contributions, and 13% in indirect taxes. That actually makes the burden look lighter than it really is. In their splendidly clear and amusing book, *The British Tax System* (1978) John Kay and Mervyn King did some calculations. They added up what the typical worker paid in income tax, national insurance contributions (his own and his employer's, plus the surcharge), and taxes on spending. They calculated that most people in Britain faced a marginal effective tax rate of 51%. In other words, the effective burden on each additional pound we earn is probably over 50 pence. Their figures left out several imposts, including rates, corporation tax, and capital taxes.

How has it happened? How is it that, without any electorate consciously voting for it, we have moved from the situation in 1939 when there were only four million taxpayers in a working population of twenty million, to a world in which almost everyone who works is eligible for tax?

There are two answers. One is that we have all (really!) become much richer; and as we have become richer we have chosen to spend a rising proportion of our extra wealth on things which the public sector provide. As the chapter on public expenditure (chapter 2) points out, government spending has grown enormously, relative to the size of the GDP. The Welfare State is not cheap: there are simply not enough rich individuals to carry the cost of social security, education and the National Health Service.

But inflation is the other part of the story. It affects different parts of the tax system in different ways. With indirect taxes, what happens depends on whether the tax is levied as a percentage or at a flat rate. VAT is levied as a percentage: and so when prices rise, the yield from VAT rises too. (In a recession, this is partly offset by the fact that when people spend less, the yield from VAT tends to fall. But that is an effect of the recession, and not of changing prices.) Flat-rate duties, such as the duty on tobacco and on alcohol, do not automatically rise in line with inflation, and so unless the Chancellor of the Exchequer deliberately announces a tax change, their real value gradually declines. An example from *The British Tax System*: in terms of 1979 prices, the duty on a bottle of standard whisky dropped from £6.77 in 1966 to £3.78 in 1979, and the duty on a packet of twenty standard tipped cigarettes fell from 58 pence to 42 pence.

But it is on income tax that the impact of inflation is most dramatic. As prices rise, most people receive pay increases which may simply keep their incomes abreast of rising prices. But these pay increases, which may do no more than maintain the purchasing power of a pay packet, also mean that people tend to find their income tax bills rising. Two things happen. The value of the allowances which all taxpayers can set off against their income tax liabilities is diminished. And the point at which people start to pay the higher rates of income tax falls in real terms. These effects go under the horrible name of 'fiscal drag'.*

One of the big landmarks in recent tax history was the passage, in 1977, of an amendment to the Finance Act sponsored by a curious alliance of two left-wing Labour MPs (Geoff Rooker and Audrey Wise) and Nigel Lawson (Conservative Financial Secretary as from 1979). This amendment required the Chancellor to raise personal tax allowances by at least as much as the rise in the retail prices index in the preceding calendar year, unless he takes a public decision not to do so. It has at long last stopped Chancellors pretending that they were not raising taxes if they left income tax allowances unchanged. (It was interesting to see Ronald Reagan's advisers counting on fiscal drag to reduce the impact of the income tax cuts which they proposed after his election as US President.)

Does the rise in the tax burden really matter? Of course, nobody much likes the feeling that half their extra income is going to the government to be spent on their behalf. Tax-cutters, to judge by events in Britain and America, win elections. But do high taxes actually damage the economy?

There is certainly a popular view that high taxes discourage people from working, or encourage them to work in unproductive parts of the economy. In the US, a gentleman called

Arthur Laffer has put forward the view that cutting taxes may raise tax revenue. Increasing taxation, he argues, diminishes the yield in three ways: by discouraging people from working longer hours or accepting promotion to higher paid jobs; by making it more attractive to live on social security; and by encouraging evasion. This view is tagged 'supply side economics'.

Sadly, most serious economic work on these propositions casts doubt on Laffer's ingenious idea that tax cuts can raise revenue. Take first the proposal that a heavy tax burden may discourage people from working. What matters here is not the average tax burden — the average amount of tax that each person pays — but the marginal rate of tax, the tax someone pays on each extra pound earned. That may be quite different from the average rate of tax. Imagine a system where income tax is 20% on all incomes up to £5000 a year, but 90% on income from £5001 up. Someone earning £5002 a year will pay an average rate of tax of approximately 20%, but will face a marginal rate of 90%. One of the most peculiar features of British income tax is that the basic rate of 30% applies to a very wide band of income. That has always meant that the average tax rate in Britain has been broadly in line with average tax rates in other industrial countries. But until the Conservatives reduced the top rate of incomes to 60% in their 1979 budget, we had uniquely high marginal rates on higher incomes.

There were many attempts, in the time of James Callaghan's Labour government, to prove that high marginal tax rates discouraged people from working harder. None succeeded in proving the point beyond a doubt. And the truth is that people may plausibly react in one of two ways to a rise in their marginal tax rate. They may say, 'It's not worth working so hard if the extra cash I make simply goes to the taxman'; or they may say, 'This rise in taxes has diminished my total income, and so I must work harder to get back to where I was'. There is at least an awful possibility that high taxes may encourage hard work.*

There seems a better case for arguing that high marginal tax rates may encourage the growth of the 'black economy'. They probably have played some part in the huge growth of fringe benefits, such as company cars, in the last few years — although there has been no sign of the growth of company cars abating since the reduction in very high marginal rates. And it is at least possible that the growth in the number of people who want to be paid in cash (a growth which is impossible to measure and hard even to establish beyond doubt) is related to the rise in the total numbers of taxpayers, rather than to the level of taxation. If a small minority of workers pay income tax (as in 1939) there are bound to be fewer evaders than if almost everyone pays it.

The reason why we have rising marginal rates of income tax in the first place is that one of the things which the tax system is supposed to do is to encourage a more equal distribution of income and wealth. One of the reasons why our tax system is so complex, indeed, is that people want taxation to achieve a number of different goals, not all of which are compatible. The goal of redistribution, for instance, is inevitably in conflict with the goal of encouraging incentive. The goal of fairness − of trying to tailor a tax system which will take each person's particular circumstances into account, before taxing him − is inevitably in conflict with that of simplicity. We could have a much simpler income tax system if we did not offer special allowances to the handicapped, to those with elderly dependents, to widows in the year of their husband's death, and to people awarded pensions in recognition of acts of gallantry. But it might also be a system which was less fair.*

Reforming the tax system is one of those projects which keeps armchair economists happy for hours. Now I want to say a bit about some of the main ways in which the tax system works badly, and about some of the most likely projects for improvement.

Most of the criticism is inevitably directed at income tax. Perhaps the most common complaints are that the income tax system is more complicated than it need be; that it overlaps with the social security system in a way which traps people in low-income jobs; and that its treatment of savings is muddled and illogical.

We have in this country a Rolls Royce system for collecting the bulk of income tax. It is designed to involve minimum work for the taxpayer − or as Kay and King put it: 'The central assumption is that the taxpayer is incompetent'. The hard work is done by employers, who deduct most income tax from the taxpayer's pay packet through the machinery of Pay As You Earn

(PAYE). This means that the vast majority of people in employment only have to fill in a simple income tax return every five years. Most industrial countries operate some sort of PAYE system. But what is almost unique about the British system, and what makes it pecularily complicated to administer, is the principle of cumulation.

Most countries make weekly or monthly deductions from income in a rough and ready way, and if the taxpayer ends up paying too much tax or too little, he claims a rebate or writes a cheque at the end of the tax year. The British system attempts to deduct exactly the right amount of tax during the year and avoid any need for end-year assessment — which is why most taxpayers only have to fill in tax returns every five years. But to do this, it is necessary to keep a cumulative tax record throughout the year for every taxpayer. If a man stops working halfway through the tax year, he will shortly receive a tax rebate to take account of the fact that he overpaid during the early part of the year. Most other countries would simply stop collecting tax from him, and make any adjustments when the final sums are done at the end of the year.

The Inland Revenue argues that the British taxpayer would be unhappy with a system which involved him in more work, or which did not adjust tax deducted in this sophisticated way. Who would want to be landed with a large bill for unpaid tax at the end of the fiscal year? But the principle of cumulation is undoubtedly one reason why the Inland Revenue employs roughly four times as many staff, relative to the number of taxpayers, as the US Internal Revenue service. Most proposals for changing the tax system assume that sooner or later we will move closer to a system of self-assessment, where the individual taxpayer has the job of checking his or her allowances, and the responsibility for settling up with the tax authorities. That would mean more work for most of us, but it might also push the authorities towards devising a tax system which is easier to understand. If it did not (or even if it did) it would inevitably — like most tax changes — mean more work for accountants!

So much for the administration of income tax. But its structure also causes problems. One of the most important is the way in which it overlaps with social security benefits. It is perfectly possible for someone to be simultaneously receiving Family Income Supplement and paying income tax and national insurance contributions. Because of the way in which means-tested benefits are withdrawn as income rises, some poor families can, at least theoretically, face marginal tax rates of over 100%. In other words, if their earnings rise by a few extra pounds, they lose more than the whole increase through the withdrawal of benefits and the effect of taxation.

When Margaret Thatcher was fighting the 1979 general election, there was a great deal of talk about the disincentive effects of high marginal tax rates on people with very big salaries, but much less about the effect on people with very low pay. But for them the disincentive effects may well be greater, if only because the badly paid are likely to be doing jobs which are much less rewarding in other ways. You might put up with a marginal tax rate of 83% for the fun, or social status, of running a large public company; agricultural labourers and cemetery workers do not have those non-financial rewards.*

However, getting rid of the 'poverty trap' will not be easy. There is an inevitable conflict between schemes which concentrate on giving the largest possible amount of financial help to the very poor, and schemes which concentrate on a smooth band of marginal tax rates as the poor move up the income scale.

The crux of the problem is this. The best way to concentrate on helping the poor is to apply a means test: to say that there will be social security benefits available for everyone whose income falls below a certain level — and not for anyone else. Suppose, in a simplified case, that income level is £40 a week. As soon as someone takes a job which pays £40.01 a week, he loses every penny of benefit. That would be the ultimate poverty trap.

The other extreme would be to try to tax everyone on a gently rising curve of marginal tax rates. The government might, for instance, decide to scrap all existing social security benefits and give everyone in the country £40 a week, and then tax everyone 50% of their income. Such a tax scheme, with the same marginal rate for everyone on every £1, would involve no poverty trap at all. But it would be vastly more expensive than the first scheme. For it would involve the government in giving

40

£40 a week to a lot of people earning more than that amount, as well as to the poor, and yet would only recoup at most half, 50%, of each £40 handed out. All schemes to deal with poverty lie somewhere between these two extremes. Negative income tax and tax credits are a version of the latter; our present system, of the former.*

The taxation of savings poses a different set of problems. At the moment, we tax savings in a bewildering variety of ways. This was one of the points made forcefully by the committee set up by the Institute for Fiscal Studies under James Meade to look at the structure and reform of direct taxation (Meade, 1978). Meade drew attention to the wild variations in the rate of tax on savings. There are two particular oddities.

First, capital gains are not taxed as income. The maximum rate is 30%, the same as the basic rate of income tax. So anyone who is taxed at a higher marginal rate has an incentive to make sure that he reaps the rewards of an investment in the form of a capital gain, rather than an interest payment or a dividend. Second, there are a number of forms of saving which attract very favourable tax treatment. If you put your savings into the purchase of a large house, you will not only be given tax relief on interest payments on a mortgage of up to £25,000; you will pay no capital gains when you sell it. Life assurance policies and pension funds also get special treatment. It is not surprising that these three forms of savings accounted for nearly 90% of all savings in the UK between 1972 and 1976, compared with less than 60% in the US. Nor is it surprising that government securities, which also get favourable tax treatment, now account for nearly 90% of investment in the long-term capital market.

There is a clear case for trying to bring the tax treatment of different kinds of savings into line in some way. It is now widely believed that the favourable tax treatment of the large financial institutions has helped to discriminate against small businesses. Ultimately, the government will have to choose between giving all savings some sort of harmonized tax relief: or bringing income from savings back into the tax net. The second option would imply getting rid of tax relief on mortgage interest, taxing capital gains as ordinary income and removing the tax relief on life assurance premiums.

That might be part of a general policy to broaden the tax base: the kinds of income and the range of spending subject to taxation. Obviously the wider the tax base, the lower average tax rates have to be. As Kay and King point out, less than half of all UK income is subject to income tax, and little over half of all consumer spending is subject to VAT.

But the other option would be to follow the suggestion of the Meade Committee and look for a way of taxing income when it is spent, rather than when it is saved. The trouble with VAT is that it takes no account of the circumstances of the people who pay it. Designing an expenditure tax which taxed big spenders proportionately more heavily than the average man would — under the current system — be an administrative nightmare. But once the operations of the Inland Revenue are finally transferred to computer, and if the British public could be persuaded to accept self-assessment, it might become possible.

There remain two other serious gaps in our tax system. One is the taxation of companies; the other, the treatment of wealth. The taxation of companies is a large and elaborate problem. The main difficulty is to find a way of adjusting for the distorting effect of inflation on company profits. I do not propose to spell it out in detail, but put simply, the difficulty is this: suppose a company making cars buys a stock of steel. The value of the steel then rises, because of inflation. On paper, that appears as a profit on the purchase of the steel. In practice, of course, the company has to replace the steel at the new higher price to make the next batch of cars. In current price terms — as opposed to historic cost terms — it has made no profit at all.

As it stands, corporation tax is imposed on a company's profits measured at historic cost. If that had really happened for the past inflationary decade, large chunks of British industry would by now belong to the Inland Revenue. In fact, a scheme of stock relief was introduced in 1974. It was meant as an emergency measure; it lasted, with variations, much longer than anyone expected. Because the accountancy profession has taken so long to agree on a way of presenting company accounts to reflect the effects of inflation, it has been impossible to re-vamp corporation tax to allow for rising prices.

The other gap is the taxation of wealth. We don't do it.

Unless you count local authority rates, and a capital gains tax which does not distinguish between pure gains and gains which merely keep pace with inflation, unless you count these, the taxation of wealth is virtually non-existent. Capital Transfer Tax actually raises less revenue than estate duty used to do.

There are three main approaches to the taxation of wealth. It can be taxed when it generates income, as for example, in the case of the taxation of share dividends. It can be taxed when it changes hands, as in the case of stamp duty, estate duty or Capital Transfer Tax. Or one can simply tax its ownership − as with wealth tax or rates − on the grounds that the mere possession of wealth gives certain advantages.

One of the reasons why the taxation of wealth has attracted more attention in recent years is the growing awareness that wealth is less evenly distributed than income in Britain. The degree of inequality is less easy to measure for wealth than for income. Personal income is usually measured either before income tax or after it − though it is also possible to add in social security benefits and to try to impute benefit from public sector services, such as free health care and free education. Obviously, income is much less evenly distributed if measured in gross (pre-tax) terms than if measured after making allowance for the redistributive effect of income tax, social benefits and public services.

But measuring the distribution of wealth is even more complicated. Most people would probably accept that wealth should not just be defined in terms of stocks and shares, ownership of agricultural land and large houses, but should include all owner-occupied houses in some way or other. Even those of us who do not live in a stately home still hold a great deal of our physical wealth in the form of a car, a washing machine, a cooker or a three-piece sitting-room suite. Should those count as wealth? Things start to look even more complicated when you add in financial claims. Most people would think the ownership of shares was a form of wealth. Perhaps, then, membership of an occupational pension should also count as wealth − it is, after all, a claim on income in old age, even though it cannot be sold. And if occupational pension schemes count towards wealth, then perhaps, by analogy, so should the rights which most of us have to a state pension.

43

But once you reach this stage, wealth is much more evenly distributed across the population than it is if you take a simpler and more obvious measure. The Royal Commission on the Distribution of Income and Wealth commented on the subject in its fourth report (Cmnd 6626). If one took the narrowest definition of wealth, making no allowance for pension rights, it looked as though the wealthiest 1% of the population owned about 25% of personal wealth. If one made allowance for state and occupational pension rights, the wealthiest 1% owned about 14% of all personal wealth.

Even that takes no account of intangible and probably immeasureable forms of 'wealth' such as a good education or training; or membership of a profession or trade union with restricted entry. People who enjoy any of these are arguably 'wealthy' in that they have greater potential earning power. But a more important point is that the distribution of wealth, even on the broadest measure, is still considerably less even than the distribution of personal incomes after tax. The top 1% of recipients of personal incomes after tax accounted for just over 4% of the total.

So wealth is apparently much less evenly distributed than income. That does not bother Conservative tax reformers much; but it has led Labour politicians (and others) to call for two particular alterations in the tax regime. One is the taxation of holdings of wealth; the other the more efficient taxation of transfers of wealth.

The taxation of holdings of wealth implies a wealth tax. A wealth tax is one of the oldest kinds of imposts: the complex problem of assessment did not exist when you simply looked at the numbers of fields, servants and cattle an individual owned. Most European countries have had a wealth tax since the start of this century: although only the Republic of Ireland has introduced one recently. For to operate a wealth tax which is more than a gesture is extremely difficult. Think of some of the problems. It is a great deal easier to hide jewellery from the taxman than stocks and shares: a wealth tax might encourage people to put their cash into diamond necklaces instead of industrial investment. The man who owned a large house might have very little income out of which to pay his wealth tax assessment; should he be taxed to the point where he has to borrow against the value of his house to pay? Agricultural land, small businesses and forestry plantations may be simultaneously a form of personal wealth and an enterprise. How should a wealth tax treat them?

The taxation of holdings of wealth is not beyond the wit of man, but it is very difficult. Most governments have prefered to settle for taxing income from wealth, or taxing the stuff when it changes hands. There is some logic in this: the best chance of being wealthy is to have wealthy parents. Both these policies raise some of the difficulties of a wealth tax. Until 1974 transfers of wealth were taxed mainly at death, through estate duty. Anyone who wanted to avoid paying tax simply had to make sure he transferred his estate to his heirs some time before his death. Capital Transfer Tax in theory taxes transfers of wealth during the life of the donor, as well as bequests. But it has become full of exceptions and special cases, on which lower duty is charged.

Probably the most sensible alternative to Capital Transfer Tax would be a tax on the recipients of gifts and bequests, rather than on the donors. Such a reform, an 'accessions tax', could be made progressive: the more an individual received over the year or indeed over his lifetime, the higher the rate at which each new receipt could be taxed. This would have the great advantage of actively encouraging individuals who wanted to minimize the tax burden on the estate they were handing on to give it to people who were not already wealthy, rather than to those who were.

People would, of course, still lobby for special treatment for small businesses, agricultural land, forests and works of art. To give in to demands like these does not necessarily help businessmen, farmers, and foresters. Take the case of agricultural land. If it is exempted from tax, then wealthy people who want to avoid tax on their wealth will switch some of their assets into farms. Farmers who happen to own their land will make a windfall gain − which, however, they will only be able to realize by selling their land to tax-dodging tycoons and moving to Hampstead. Young farmers will find it much more expensive to buy land of their own. And tax revenue will be lower than it would otherwise have been.

But that is always the problem with altering the tax system. It is precisely because tax reform alters the distribution of income that it so rarely takes place. For tax reform is almost always expensive: it is safer to leave some people with more money and some with a lot more money, if you are a politician, than to leave some with less and some with more.

4 De-industrialization: have the jobs gone for ever?

In all the mature industrial economies, a similar and disturbing trend has appeared in the past decade. The growth of jobs in manufacturing has slowed down, halted, or gone into reverse. The cause is not the recession, although of course the recession has made it worse. And while in some countries the trend has only become apparent since the sharp rise of oil prices in the early 1970s, in others — including Britain — it was already evident towards the end of the 1960s.

In Britain, 'de-industrialization' has been apparent for longer than almost anywhere else. Between 1960 and the end of 1980, the number of people employed in manufacturing fell from 8.2 million to just over 6.3 million. From right back in the middle of the 1950s, the job market has seen first a fall in manufacturing employment in proportional terms, and more recently, an absolute decline.

The decline has been blamed on the growth of the public sector (and so had a powerful influence on the policies of the 1979 Conservative government) and it has been blamed on foreign competition (and so influenced the Labour party's enthusiasm for import controls). It has been blamed on North Sea oil and on new technology — although neither can easily explain a change which began so long ago. It has been blamed on the rise of the newly industrialized nations — Brazil and Mexico, Taiwan, the Philippines, and Korea — although these countries still have only a tiny share of total world trade in manufactures. It has caused some people to dread an industrial wasteland, with millions of unemployed, and others to dream of a new future in which everyone works for education or the health service while a few button-pushers keep the wheels of a totally automated manufacturing industry still turning.

This chapter first looks at the phenomenon of de-industrialization: at what has happened here and abroad. It then picks through the various explanations, and ends by hazarding a guess about whether the future is really as bleak as the general consensus seems to be.

Over the past fifteen years, manufacturing has become relatively less and less important in the total of economic activity. In 1965 manufacturing represented 34% of the value of total output. It had been growing in importance since the start of the decade. But by the early 1970s, the share had declined to around 30% and by 1980 it was probably less than 25% of the whole economy. The decline was then sharply accentuated by the recession: during the twelve-month period up to the fourth quarter of 1980, manufacturing production dropped by about 15%, the largest drop in any such period since the war. Over the same year, the workforce in manufacturing shrank by 10% compared with the average the previous year.

But it is the decline in jobs which most worries people. Up to 1966, the absolute numbers employed in manufacturing were still rising. That year, they hit a peak for the UK of 8.6 million. Ten years later, more than 1.3 million people had left manufacturing industry. Over the same period, the numbers employed in private services fluctuated but did not grow. The numbers employed in the public services rose steadily, although by not quite as much as the fall in jobs in manufacturing and other production industries.

Side by side with this change, another has been taking place. Manufacturing is predominantly an employer of men. In the decade between 1966 and 1976, 1.4 million jobs for men in production industries disappeared. Jobs for women in industry also vanished — but because fewer women were employed in the first place, fewer jobs went. The services, and particularly the public services, are large employers of women. So in the same decade, the public sector generated just over a million new jobs for women. The private sector service industries generated some jobs for women, too. But new jobs for men in public sector service industries were more than outweighed by the loss of jobs for men in private sector services. One final aspect of the change is important: most of the jobs which have vanished have been full-time jobs. Most of the new jobs have been part-time jobs.*

Now this curious transformation of the economy has not been unique to Britain. Taking the years between 1960 and 1975, one finds that the US, Sweden, Holland, and Belgium have all seen steady declines in the proportion of total employment in manufacturing. By contrast, the proportion in Japan, Germany, and Italy has risen – although in all three, the rate of growth faltered by the middle 1970s. From the evidence of other economies, it looks as though most of them underwent some change in the early 1970s which resulted in a slowdown and then a decline in the growth of manufacturing employment as a proportion of all jobs. De-industrialization is by no means a purely British experience.

One of the first explanations of de-industrialization to gain popularity was put forward by Robert Bacon and Walter Eltis in a series of articles in *The Sunday Times* in November 1974. They laid the blame for the contraction of manufacturing on excessive government spending. At one level, their hypothesis was simply that the creation of jobs in the public sector had diverted manpower from the private sector. But this argument quickly evolved into a more sophisticated contention that the increasing claims of government had reduced the proportion of output available for consumption by the rest of the community.

The simplest version of the Bacon and Eltis thesis has never looked very convincing. It is hard to argue that successive public sector expansions have crippled industry by absorbing labour which manufacturing might otherwise have employed: as we have seen, it is men's jobs which have been mainly lost in manufacturing, while the 1970s expansion of the public sector largely created women's jobs. Nor is it easy to believe that the private sector was held back by a shortage of funds – simply 'crowded out' of the capital market. That has no doubt happened from time to time, but it is not at all clear that shortage of funds or even excessively high interest rates have been a major obstacle to

49

the expansion of manufacturing employment in the past decade and a half.*

But the more subtle explanation is more interesting. It is that the public sector (or rather, the 'non-market' sector), of the economy has tried to pre-empt a larger and larger share of the resources created by the market sector by raising taxation. Higher taxes have led workers to demand higher wages to pay for them. This has prevented the expansion of the non-market sector from squeezing consumption, but it has shifted the burden on to company profits, and on to the balance of payments. The squeeze on company profits has checked investment. The refusal of wage-earners to accept a cut in their living standards in order to pay for the expansion of the public sector has thrown the current account of the balance of payments (the 'non-oil' current account) into deficit.*

This argument, or something very like it, was the theme behind the Conservative government's first White Paper on Public Expenditure (1979) (see p. 17). There are a number of problems with it. For instance, the volume of manufacturing investment increased quite substantially through the 1960s. And in an article in the *Economic Journal* in March 1975, Mervyn King argued that there was no long-run or secular fall in the profits earned by UK manufacturing between 1950 and 1973, compared with income from employment. It seems at least possible that if the non-market sector had not expanded in the 1960s and early 1970s, the resources which it used would not have been redirected into the expansion of the market sector, but would have remained largely unused. In other words, the growth of public sector employment may have prevented an earlier rise in unemployment. The thesis is something which the Conservative government's economic policies will help to test.*

But if de-industrialization is not the fault of the growth of government, then what other explanation can there be? One possibility is that what we have seen is simply the old, familiar post-war problem of poor British competitiveness, manifested in a new form. This is rather the view which the 'new Cambridge' school of economists have developed (in the CEPG directed by Wynne Godley). It has led them to the conclusion

50

that the only hope of preserving jobs in manufacturing in Britain is to impose a general regime of import controls.

This thesis rests on the observation that it is not just in terms of its share of employment that UK manufacturing has been declining. It has also lost ground internationally, in terms of its share of world trade in manufactures and of world output of manufactures. In 1955, the UK accounted for 20% of world trade in manufactures. By 1976, that had declined to less than 9%. Between 1960 and 1975, the UK share of world manufacturing output at constant prices fell from nearly 10% to less than 6%.

In the 1960s, everyone worried about Britain's falling share of the world market. In the 1970s, everyone began to worry about Britain's falling share of its own home market. Imported manufactured goods took about 8% of the home market in 1961 and 13% ten years later. But while Britain's loss of world market share slowed down in the 1970s, import penetration accelerated. By 1976, imports were accounting for 21% of the home market for manufactured goods.

If British industry had been more successful at fending off foreign competition, then it would have been able to increase its output faster, and employment in manufacturing would probably have fallen much less rapidly than it has. But why has British industry found it so hard to compete? There are two answers, one old and one new.

Until the late 1970s, there was quite a lot of evidence that the problem was *not* that British manufactures were too expensive, compared with foreign competition. Over the long run, exchange rate changes – the devaluation of the pound and the appreciation of the currencies of our strongest competitors – roughly balanced the tendency of British costs to rise faster than those of other countries. So it looks as though Britain's failure to compete successfully in the world market and at home is the result of something other than price.

The UK car industry epitomizes the problem. It is one of the industries where world market share has been lost most dramatically, where imports have grown fastest, and where the decline in labour has been most striking. Yet British cars have not, over most of the past fifteen years, been wildly over-priced compared with foreign competitors. They seem to have suffered

51

from a reputation for poor reliability, manufacturers' inability to keep delivery dates, bad distribution of spare parts, and unimaginative design. These problems are not simply the result of low investment, or bad labour relations, or restrictive practices and overmanning, or the low status of middle management and the poor pay of production engineers in Britain. But all these things put together have produced an industry incapable of holding its own against the better-organized industries of Japan, or West Germany, or the US.

That is the old problem of competitiveness. But of course, the late 1970s saw the emergence of a new one. By the end of 1980, it was no longer true that the exchange rate compensated firms for loss of competitiveness. From a peak in 1977, UK competitiveness fell by 65% by the end of 1980. The appreciation of the pound coincided with a rapid rise in British labour costs, faster than in most other industrial countries. As a result, British firms lost out twice over.*

There are two possible explanations for this massive loss of competitiveness. One blames it on interest rates. The other blames it on North Sea oil.

The interest rate theory is the simplest. The Conservative government's monetary policy, it argues, has had as its main weapon an unprecedentedly high level of interest rates. In the summer of 1980, British interest rates were the highest in the industrial world. Combine that with a country self-sufficient in oil, and with a Prime Minister widely admired by foreign bankers for her toughness, and who could wonder at sterling's appreciation?*

But others point out that it was hard to explain all of sterling's strength in terms of interest rates. Between summer 1980 and the end of that year, UK interest rates moved from a level 6% above comparable US rates to a level 6% below; but the pound continued to appreciate. An alternative school of thought argues that an inevitable consequence of Britain's self-sufficiency in oil will be a relative decline in the manufacturing sector − and that the strong exchange rate is the mechanism which brings this about.

This line of argument begins by pointing out that the balance of payments must always balance. If one part of it runs a bigger

52

surplus, then sheer accounting dictates that another part must run a larger deficit – or a smaller surplus – to match it. Britain's possession of North Sea oil inevitably means that the energy account of the balance of payments will be strengthened. Something, somewhere else, has to make room. In the medium term, there are two possibilities. Either the rest of the current account can deteriorate – we can import more or export less – or the capital account can move further into deficit, reflecting an outflow of investment from the country. Because these changes will not take place overnight, the immediate effect of an improvement in the oil balance will be a rise in the value of the pound. That will automatically begin the work of increasing imports and reducing exports which will allow the adjustment to take place through the current account.*

But because most of the things we export are finished manufactured goods, it is manufacturing which will bear the brunt of this adjustment. Allow sterling to appreciate unchecked, and the inevitable consequence of our possession of North Sea oil will be a smaller manufacturing sector than we would otherwise have had. There are only two ways to half the appreciation. One is to encourage an outflow of capital – to invest the proceeds of North Sea oil abroad. That would put the burden of adjustment on the capital account of the balance of payments, and would mean that when the oil ran out, we might be able to live on the earnings from our investments abroad. The only alternative is to expand the economy – to try to create demand at home which will offset the loss of demand for our manufactures overseas.

Each course has its drawbacks. There is a widely held view that more investment abroad means less capital for British industry. This is nonsense: what holds back investment in Britain is the poor rate of return which investors can earn on their money, and that in turn is a reflection of the poor profitability of British industry. But investing abroad means taking a risk that the investment will be safe, and that its profits will eventually come back to Britain. Expanding the economy to boost demand faces a different set of risks: the danger that inflation might once again take off, for instance, and the danger that no expansion could be large enough to offset the

53

impact on the balance of payments of another big jump in the price of oil.

There is one other policy option which has become politically increasingly seductive: the imposition of import controls. The CEPG has advocated them as the only hope of restoring full employment and the competitiveness of British industry. What the CEPG has in mind is a system of universal controls on the imports of finished manufactured goods, to prevent any further increase in the volume of imports. This, it argues, would allow British manufacturers to expand their own output, and to produce on a scale which would make them competitive once again. Only by allowing rapid expansion, argues the CEPG, can we hope to achieve a big rise in productivity: high unemployment makes workers more resistant to new investment and new production methods.

There are a number of objections to this argument. First, if the growth of imports were checked, and the current account of the balance of payments thus became stronger, it seems probable that sterling would appreciate further and the competitiveness of British exports would deteriorate still more. Second, it is very hard to imagine that the rest of the world would be prepared to accept a regime of general import controls in Britain without retaliating. After all, most other industrial countries are struggling with large deficits, the result of having to cope with importing expensive oil: Britain is almost the only industrial country self-sufficient in oil. Quite apart from being a flagrant breach of our treaty obligations to our Common Market partners, import controls would reduce the market for other countries' exports.

The reply of the CEPG to these two objections is a subtle one. Their scheme involves controls which would maintain, not diminish, the size of the British market for imports. If we continued to buy as many imports of finished manufactures as before — though out of higher incomes — sterling would not be driven up, and the market of our trading partners would not be damaged.

Whether or not you accept this scheme depends on the view you take of two issues. The first is economic. The CEPG case rests on the argument that the reason for Britain's poor competitiveness lies in the slow growth of our markets. Slow growth of demand breeds slow growth of supply: productivity can only expand rapidly when industry's markets are also growing quickly. Protection offers the only hope of rapid expansion at home without attracting a flood of imports — and only by rapid expansion over quite a long period can one hope to break through the vicious cycle of slow growth and poor competitiveness which has been the central economic problem in post-war Britain.

But there is another possible explanation. It may be that Britain's poor competitiveness is not basically economic. It may be that its causes lie in our attitudes to work: in poor labour relations, badly trained management, poor motivation, lack of attention to quality and detail — a host of social factors for which economists have no cure. If that is the case, then import controls, even of the sophisticated kind propounded by the CEPG, would not be a solution. They might make things worse. Arguably the pressure of foreign competition is the one thing which keeps British management on its toes. Once import controls were imposed, they would be very hard to remove — and would have to be progressively tightened, as import penetration once again began to seep into the economy.

There is a second, political issue at stake. In the other industrial countries there are also strong lobbies calling for import controls. For management and trade unions alike, import controls are a highly attractive solution. For the consumer, of course, they mean less choice and higher prices. But for companies, they offer the best hope of a quieter and more prosperous life: relief from competition from abroad. So in the US and in Germany, just as much as in the UK, there are companies and workers clamouring for protection from Japanese cars and Taiwanese shirts. If one major country gives way to these demands — even in the pursuit of a sophisticated scheme like that put forward by the CEPG — it will become virtually impossible for other governments to continue to resist. The result will be a sharp reduction in the size of world markets. It was just such a spread of protectionism which ensured the spread of the pre-war depression and reinforced its severity.*

But the problem of the strong pound, partly ameliorated

when US interest rates rose and oil prices fell, has merely aggravated the decline of manufacturing employment. If one tries to abstract from the impact of the recession and the appreciation, there is an agnostic question which ought to be put. Does the decline in manufacturing employment really matter?

It is, after all, perfectly possible for jobs in manufacturing to contract at a time when output in manufacturing is growing. Indeed, this is exactly what happened between the end of 1965 and the end of 1977. Jobs in UK manufacturing fell by 15%, while output rose by 16%. If productivity increases in an economy whichis not growing very fast, then a decline in jobs in manufacturing is almost inevitable. It is precisely this which worries people about the 'new technology' — the possibility of enormous increases in productivity caused by investment in micro-electronics, replacing the jobs of millions of workers.

But if our problem were only a large rise in productivity, we would have much less to worry about. It would be easy to create jobs elsewhere in the economy to absorb the workers shed by manufacturing. Of course, individuals might have very serious difficulties in changing their job. But at least the jobs would be there.

Consider as an analogy what has happened to agriculture in this country. In 1801, an estimated 36% of the occupied population of Britain worked in agriculture. That is a good deal more than the 30% of the working population now occupied in the manufacturing industry. By 1851, the proportion of the workforces in agriculture had dropped to 22%; by 1871 to 15%; and by the turn of the century to 9%. The decline of employment in agriculture was one of the most dramatic developments of the nineteenth century. But the workers found jobs, the countryside has not returned to uncultivated wilderness, and even today, with less than 3% of the working population down on the farm, we still manage to produce roughly half our food requirements.

Now you might argue, of course, that this was a move from low productivity agriculture into higher productivity manufacturing. Services are generally less productive than manufacturing. But in terms of the foreign balance — which is what matters in this debate — the analogy holds.

There is no logical reason why manufacturing should not go the way that agriculture has gone. We might well end up earning a surplus on current account from a manufacturing industry whose output will be larger than that of today, but which employs only a handful of the working population. Where would all the others work?*

Well, the experience of the past decades has suggested that the service industries have an almost unlimited ability to absorb labour. Part of the reason is that productivity means something different in most service industries from its meaning in manufacturing. An improvement in the quality of medical care almost inevitably means more doctors, more nurses and more ancillary staff. An improvement in service in a restaurant means more waiters, if not more cooks. An improvement in the administration of local authority planning regulations means more staff in the council planning department. It is extremely difficult, in many services, to maintain the quality of output at the same time as increasing productivity.

The main problem with the service industries, in the past twenty years, has been that the fastest growing areas of employment have been in the public sector. To pay for them, the burden of taxation has had to increase. This may well have been partly a response of the tax system to public demand. As people grow richer, they want to spend a rising proportion of their incomes on better health care and better education. If these are provided mainly through the public sector, a rise in the tax burden may, in a sense, be just what people want.*

But it should be clear from chapters 2 and 3 that it will be hard to expand the public services from taxpayers' money alone from now on. If the services are to resume their growth, they will have to be financed partly out of private funds. That means finding ways of expanding health care and improving the quality of education without dismantling the welfare state – an issue touched on at the end of chapter 2.*

Even if we find a way of beating that problem, we can still not rely on the service industries to generate the contribution to the balance of payments which manufacturing fails to make. For manufacturing is still a much bigger export earner than private services, earning roughly twice as much foreign currency, and the ratio between the two has changed very little in recent years. So although we seem to be better at selling services abroad than at selling manufactures, we would need a very big increase in the total sales of private services abroad to offset a fairly small decline in manufacturing exports.

To sum up, de-industrialization appears to be a new name for the old British problem of uncompetitive manufacturing. It is a problem which has been exacerbated by the appreciation of sterling. Its causes lie in the structure of British industry, in the quality of management and the tradition of labour relations. There are no easy cures: certainly not public spending cuts, planning agreements or import controls. If manufacturing industry became more competitive, it might still shed jobs, but at least it would be easier for the rest of the economy to replace them.*

5 The City: has it failed British industry?

We all know by now that Britain's economy has grown more slowly in the post-war period than that of any other important industrial country. We all know, too — because the City of London frequently tells us — that one of the few industries in which we excel by world standards is the provision of financial services. So it is not surprising if people often wonder whether, in some sense or other, the City is responsible for Britain's poor industrial performance.

Indeed it was to answer just that question — and to head off attempts by left-wing members of the Labour party to force the government to nationalize the clearing banks — that James Callaghan, when he was Prime Minister, set up a committee under Harold Wilson to review the function of the financial institutions. This chapter draws heavily on that committee's report, which was published in 1980 (Cmnd 7937) and which is quite simply the best work for two decades on the workings of the financial markets.

In looking at the question of whether the City has in some sense 'failed' the rest of the economy, this chapter starts with a brief sketch of what goes on in the financial markets, and of the main changes which have been taking place. It inevitably looks, in particular, at the rise and the responsibilities of the pension funds and life assurance companies.

It takes very few figures to prove that the City of London is a remarkable place. Its foreign exchange earnings per head are double those of British manufacturing industry. It boasts the world's largest insurance market, its largest foreign exchange market, its main Eurocurrency market, and it is the dominant influence in more commodities than any other financial centre. Its stock exchange does not have the largest turnover in the world; that distinction goes to New York and Tokyo before London. But there are more companies and more overseas securities quoted on the London stock exchange than on any other, and it does almost as much business as all the other stock exchanges in Europe combined. There are more American banks in London than in New York, and more banks in London than in any other city in the world.

Some of the City's institutions — the commodity markets, for instance, or the insurance markets — are in business mainly to provide services for industry, either in Britain or abroad. But the central core of the City's business is the channelling of savings into investment. The savings may be yours and mine, or they may be those of a Middle Eastern oil exporting country. The investment may be your home improvement loan; or it may be a new factory for a Midlands industrial giant; or it may be a foreign government borrowing to cope with a balance of payments deficit. The recycling of money is the mainstay of the financial institutions which are what most people have in mind when they refer to the 'City'.

What all these financial institutions are in business to do is to collect money from savers in one form, and to lend it to borrowers in another. Most financial institutions collect savings in small parcels and lend them out in larger ones. For instance, it takes (on average) the building society deposits of half a dozen individuals to put together a typical mortgage. But that is not the only way in which a saver's money is transformed. Many institutions — those which specialize in taking deposits — borrow money short-term and lend in the long-term. For instance, more than a third of the sterling funds of the clearing banks are collected through current accounts (from which the cash can be withdrawn on demand) and about three-quarters through deposits which can be withdrawn at less than three months' notice. But a growing proportion of their lending — over 40% of the total — is in the form of term loans, running for between two and seven years.

One of the functions which most financial institutions perform for the saver who puts his money into them is to spread the risks of his investment. If you lend your money to me — or use all your savings to buy shares in my company — you are taking a much greater risk than if you invest your spare cash in a unit trust which in turn parcels it together with the savings of thousands of other people and spreads the investment between a hundred different company shares. In theory, this capacity to spread risks should make investment through a financial institution safer than investment directly by an individual. But, just as the risks of losing the money are reduced, so the chances of dramatic rewards are also diminished.

Now what do financial institutions do with the money with which savers entrust them? Broadly speaking, they use it in one of two ways. They may make loans, or they may invest in equity. Of course, you and I can do one or other with our own cash: these are simply the two obvious alternatives for investing savings.

There are important differences between the two. A loan is usually made for a fixed period, at the end of which it may be withdrawn or renewed. It is usually made on the assumption that it will be repaid, and the reward for making the loan is normally no more than the payment of a rate of interest. The rate of interest may be high or low, it may fluctuate or be fixed, but it is paid at a specified rate whether the purpose for which the money has been borrowed is a fantastic success or a dismal failure.

An equity investment is quite a different matter. The most familiar equity investment is the purchase of a share in a company. First, it is not an investment for a fixed period of time. Thanks to the existence of the stock exchange, someone who has made an equity investment in a firm may sell it to someone else, but the company in which the share is held does not have to buy it back, or repay the money. The element of risk — and conversely of reward — is much greater in an equity investment than in making a loan. The reward is a share of the profits of the enterprise: the risk is total loss. From a borrower's point of view, loans and equity have different advantages. If an enterprise is a success, the borrower who has raised a large part of the capital through equity may regret having to distribute a large chunk of the profits to his backers. But if an enterprise does badly, the interest on loans will still have to be paid at regular intervals, while a company can always refuse to pay out a dividend.*

Now the financial institutions are, as I have said, the middle link in a chain which passes some savings to some borrowers. They are not the only link: people buy shares directly in companies, lend money directly to their friends, buy premium bonds in a post office and thus lend directly to the government. But they have become, in the years since the Second World War, increasingly important. There are a number of reasons for this change, some general and some particular.

First, there has been a dramatic rise in saving over the past twenty years. The rise has not taken place in *all* saving, which remains almost exactly the same as a proportion of GDP as it was by the mid 1960s. But personal saving has more than doubled as a proportion of GDP, while there has been a steady decline in company saving (which is another way of saying that retained profits have fallen) and since 1973 there has been a sharp fall in saving by the public sector (which is another way of describing the sharp increase in the public sector financial deficit).*

But while the pattern of saving has changed dramatically, the pattern of investment has not. Investment by both the public sector and companies between 1973 and 1977 was more or less identical, as a proportion of GDP, to the share of each between 1963 and 1967. The implication of a relatively stable investment pattern and a changing pattern of savings has been to increase the work that the financial system has to do to shift money between one part of the economy and another. In the words of the Wilson report, 'The domestic recycling of funds has grown enormously, and has been just as important as the better known international recycling problem'.

The rise of savings at a time of rising inflation has surprised economists. Economic theory in the past has tended to assume that inflation would lead to lower savings, but now it looks as if people try to keep their savings in real terms in a more or less constant ratio with their income. If their incomes rise, so will their savings. An alternative explanation might be that people set their targets for savings not in terms of cash but of the goods which they want to be able to buy. So if the price of, say, holidays abroad goes up, people will try to save more.*

It also seems that we like to have our savings in a fairly accessible form, such as bank and building society deposits. Again this conflicts with traditional economic theory, which predicts that when inflation is rapidly eroding the purchasing power of money, people will prefer to buy goods before the price goes up further − be they a new washing machine or a Picasso − rather than save money in, say, a building society. Yet we have chosen to save more rather than to spend. Perhaps we have simply been confused by the fact that interest rates have been at record heights − even though they have frequently been negative in real terms.*

The resulting huge increase in personal sector savings has benefited some financial institutions more than others, with the most dramatic development being the growth over the past two decades of pension funds and life assurance, and the transformation of building societies. About half of the personal sector's additions to its pool of savings through the mid 1970s went into short-term deposits, mainly with banks and with building societies. But the building societies took more than twice as large a share of the increase in personal sector deposits as did the banks. They made even bigger inroads on the share of national savings and of the savings banks. Remember the days when everyone had a Post Office savings account? Today, the sort of people who once kept most of their spare cash in the Post Office keep it with the Halifax or with Nationwide instead. The building societies have become not just one of the main ways that individuals save: they have become the largest source of loans to individuals. In some recent years, their loans to housebuyers have been bigger than bank lending to industrial and commercial companies.

There are a number of reasons for the meteoric growth of the building societies. The most important is probably the sheer popularity of home ownership. Approximately 80% of the assets of the building societies are in the form of mortgages (almost all the rest are either lent to the public sector or held in cash). Property is the investment which, over the years, has kept pace best with inflation. Home ownership is encouraged by the tax system in a number of ways: there is no capital gains tax on selling an owner-occupied house, and the interest payments on a mortgage are tax-deductible. No other investment is treated so favourably by the tax system*

Building societies themselves enjoy some unique advantages: the special system for taxing the interest they pay through one composite rate allows them to offer a slightly higher rate of interest than the banks, and they have not been subject to the battery of controls which successive governments have periodically applied to the clearing banks. But the societies have also faced weaker trade unions than the banks, which has meant that they have been able to stay open for longer hours and on Saturday mornings. And they perform a much less complicated function than the banks. It is far simpler to lend on a modern house than to assess the credit-worthiness of a small new company. That has helped to keep their staff costs and overheads much lower than those of the banks.

Individuals in the mid 1970s put roughly half their additional savings into longer-term investment. Some went into buying national savings certificates or gilts; some into unit trusts or investment trusts or local authorities; but most − about 35% of additions to the pool of personal savings between 1973 and 1977 − went into savings through life assurance and pension funds. With this change went a dramatic alteration in the ownership of company shares. The private individual, for the past twenty years, has been steadily running down his direct holdings of company shares and buying them through an institution instead. In some cases, this gives him a tax advantage: in all cases, it spreads the risk.

A few figures illustrate what has happened. The proportion of all UK listed shares owned by individual fell from 66% in 1957 to about 32% at the end of 1978. Meanwhile, the proportion owned by financial institutions climbed from 21% at the end of 1957 to 50% − precisely half − by the end of 1978. Within this total, the pension funds have grown largest: they now own 20% of all listed UK ordinary shares, with the insurance companies owning a further 17%. Both are also large holders of British government debt: at the end of 1978, insurance companies owned 29% of all non-official holdings of gilts, while the pension funds owned 16%.*

The pension funds and life assurance companies are not the only financial institutions through which individuals save long-term, but they have become far and away the most important. In 1978, the net inflow into life funds was £4 billion, and into pension funds £3.7 billion. By contrast there was no net inflow into investment trusts, and unit trusts grew by only £0.2 billion.

There are two main ways of running a pension fund. Smaller companies often hand over the job of deciding what to invest and where to a specialist financial institution − usually a life assurance company such as Legal and General or the Prudential. Larger firms often have a self-administered fund, presided over by a group of trustees and run by managers whom they appoint. This is how the pension funds of all the nationalized industries, local authorities and large companies work.

Life assurance is a different sort of service from non-life or general insurance. Non-life insurance means covering an individual or company against a specific risk − insuring a car against theft, for instance. The company only pays out money if the car is stolen. Only a small part of life assurance (known as 'term life') offers *in*surance of this kind: offering to pay out a sum of money in the event of a person's death. Most life assurance is a form of saving: a tiny part of the premiums which policy holders pay go to cover the risk of their dying early, while the rest is an investment to be paid out at a later date.

Most ordinary insurance companies − the household names like the Royal or Guardian Royal Exchange − handle both non-life insurance and life assurance. But some companies, such as Legal and General and the National Provident Institution, specialize in life assurance. They sell life policies to individuals (for whom they usually represent a form of long-term saving for old age) and they manage pension funds for companies.

The rise of pension funds and life assurance has been more impressive in Britain than in any other major industrial country.

In the mid 1970s the financial surplus of the household sector — its saving minus its investment — grew as a proportion of GDP by a bit more than in the US, France, or Germany but by less than in Japan. But savings through life assurance and pension funds were dramatically greater as a proportion of GDP in the UK — almost twice as much as the nearest rival, the US, and nearly three times as large as in West Germany.

The reason may be partly that savers prefer to spread their risks by investing through an institution rather than buying company shares directly. But that is only a small part of the story. There has been a large rise in the numbers of people covered by occupational pensions. Again, that is only a small part of the story. Most of the rise, from under 3 million employees in 1936 to 10 million in 1953, took place earlier, and between 1953 and 1975 the pension funds added only another $1\frac{1}{2}$ million or so employees to their books.

But while the membership of occupational pension schemes has not grown very fast in the last couple of decades, the level of benefit provided by pension schemes has improved considerably. There has been a steady increase in the number of employees whose pension is related to their earnings at or near retirement. There has also been a growing tendency — forced on the funds by inflation — to try to raise pensions after retirement. Most public sector employees have, either by law or by common practice, pensions which are fully protected against inflation. Hardly any private sector scheme promises or achieves full protection against inflation, but almost all now raise pensions of existing pensioners from time to time.

There are basically two ways of financing pension payments. It can either be done on a 'Pay As You Go' (PAYG) system, whereby the existing workforce effectively pays the pensions of the existing batch of pensioners; or pensions can be funded, which means that each generation of pensioners receives pensions paid out of money which they have saved through their working lives. In Britain, almost all pensions are either funded or a hybrid: only central government employees are on a fully-fledged PAYG scheme. The main argument against extending PAYG in the private sector is that it puts the livelihood of pensioners at risk if the company for which they worked goes bankrupt. In the public sector, where the employer is clearly here to stay and can draw on the bottomless purse of the taxpayer, the case against extending PAYG is more finely balanced.

But given the prevalence of funded schemes, and given the need of these schemes to pay out improving levels of benefit to a growing number of retired, it is inevitable that pension contributions have risen and that the total size of the pension funds has increased too. This has opened a new area in the old discussion of the quality of service which British industry receives from the City.

The theme of this discussion, however, has remained unchanged. Britain has grown slowly compared with other major industrial powers. British industry has invested less than industry in other countries. If that explains the slow growth, then it may be the fault of those who lend the money which finances the investment. British financial institutions, so the argument runs, have been more willing to lend abroad than to lend to British companies; they have not been prepared, like the German banks, to go on lending to companies which are going through a period of temporary difficulty, and nor have they been prepared to try to improve the quality of British management by playing a more active role in monitoring the companies in which they invest.

Now some aspects of this argument are indisputable. Since the Second World War, Britain has grown relatively slowly, its share of world trade has declined considerably, and productivity growth has been more sluggish than in most other similar countries. Through the 1970s — and indeed before — Britain's investment in manufacturing industry was relatively low. But how far this was a cause of slow growth and how far a consequence is very hard to establish.

Nor is it possible to prove that British firms have suffered from a shortage of finance. The trade-union members of the Wilson committee and Harold Wilson himself wrote a dissenting note, arguing the case for a new investment facility, jointly funded by the government and the pension and life funds, and administered by government, employers and trade unions, to channel more loans and equity finance into industry. But in spite of that, the committee unanimously concluded that

'The overwhelming view expressed in our evidence, with very few exceptions, is that the availability of external finance has not been a significant independent constraint on companies' operations, provided that they are prepared to be flexible regarding the form in which the finance is supplied'. The committee also observed, 'Industry has not felt that it has been held back by an inability to obtain external funds provided it was prepared to pay the price asked'.

The sting, however, is in the tails of those last two quotes. For there is certainly evidence that in recent years companies have not always been able to pay the price needed to obtain the finance which has been available. There has been an important change in the way that companies raise their cash.

Companies need finance whether they are expanding or not. They need finance simply in order to keep going: to pay for the stocks they hold and the work they are currently undertaking, as well as for replacing machinery and equipment as they wear out. Inflation inevitably increases the amounts of money they need, in nominal terms, just to tick over. A firm which wants to expand will need even more finance to buy new machinery and to pay for an increase in its stocks, for new advertising, marketing, trade debts, and all the overheads incurred by simply producing more goods. Since the 1960s, a bigger and bigger proportion of company finance has been simply to finance the costs of keeping going: just over half of companies' funds in 1975−9, compared with only a third in the mid 1960s.

Most company cash − about 70% over the past ten years − is generated internally: from profits earned on trading. And so the less profitable a company is, the less finance it can provide for itself and the more money it needs to find from outside. In the 1970s, British firms generated on average only 1.4 times the amount of cash they needed to cover their existing operations, compared with 2.1 times in the mid 1960s. These figures reflect what the Bank of England (in the September 1980 Quarterly Bulletin) described as 'the most serious problem in the finance of British business': the declining profitability of British firms, after allowing for the impact of inflation. Since 1974, research by the Bank suggests, the inflation-adjusted rate of return on investment has been lower than the inflation-adjusted cost of finance. For while profitability has been declining, interest rates have been rising. The effect of this has been to make companies much more reluctant to borrow long term at fixed rates of interest: through issuing debentures. Instead, the 1970s have seen a dramatic rise in the proportion of their funds which companies have had to borrow from the banks. In the 1960s, the banks provided less than half of companies' external finance; in the 1970s, they contributed about 60% and often more.

So high nominal interest rates — partly a by-product of inflation — may have made it hard for many firms to raise money, or to raise it in the way they would have liked to, during the 1970s. The clearing banks have probably become better at providing companies with money in the form they want: the growth of term lending has partly made up for the collapse of the debenture market. But the clearing banks still do not hold shares in British firms — as their counterparts in Germany do — and still do not play an active role in the way large firms are managed. By contrast, the pension funds and life assurance companies actually own a part of British industry through their shareholdings. The rise of these institutional investors has altered the argument about who in the City ought to take responsibility for the short-comings of British management.

The pension funds, said Harold Wilson, 'are so powerful that they do not know how powerful they are. They could very well be transforming the nature of our society more than any government would dare to do'. Certainly their growth has created some extraordinary paradoxes: the public sector pension funds invest in equity and property as well as in gilts, and so state employees have acquired an indirect interest in the healthy survival of the private sector while at the same time the state ownership of industry has increased spectacularly.

Some of the worries of critics of the institutional investor were dispelled by research done for the Wilson committee. The funds had been suspected of being less willing than individuals to hold shares in smaller companies. In fact, the committee found no tendency for institutional share-holdings to be concentrated among the larger firms, and it was only in the case of very small firms that institutional share-holdings were under-represented.

But that probably simply reflects the fact that many of the small firms are still largely family-owned.

Another fear was that the institutions would add to the volatility of the market in company shares. The Wilson committee found that the period for which an institution typically held a share varied widely between one kind of institution and another. At one extreme, unit trusts typically held a share for just over two years; at the other, a pension fund typically held one for six years and an insurance company for eight. That is much the same as the holding pattern of private individuals. But the committee admitted that the growth of the institutions might have made one-way markets for gilts more common — with every institution waiting for a rise in interest rates before buying — and that the same thing might eventually develop in the equity market.

But the criticisms of the institutions which appear to be more valid are that they dislike making highly risky or unusual investments, and they dislike having to intervene in a company's management. The dislike of taking risks is a matter of legal obligation as much as temperament: by law, the first concern of pension funds must be to safeguard the long-term interests of their members. 'People with savings to spare might quite reasonably be prepared to take a chance with their own money which a fund manager would not take with other people's' (paragraph 933 of the committee's report). That ought to be strong argument for diminishing the tax advantages which make it more attractive for people to save through pension funds and life assurance than to buy shares directly — or at least, for putting the tax treatment on a more equal basis.

Intervention is a more difficult issue. Gordon Richardson, the Governor of the Bank of England, like his predecessor Lord O'Brien, has devoted much effort to trying to persuade the institutional investors to exercise their responsibility for the companies in which they own shares in a more concerted and active way. The funds claim that they do a fair amount of good by stealth: publicity for their efforts may hurt a company more. The Wilson committee pointed out that a more active role by the institutions might not always be beneficial: it might make industry more cautious and less willing to undertake risky long-term projects. But from the institutions' point of view, some of them may not have much choice. For unless the number of shares quoted on the stock exchange starts to grow more rapidly than it has done in the recent past, the proportion of British industry owned by the pension funds and life assurance companies will continue to increase for some time. The larger institutions try to limit their holdings in any one company to around 5%, but the Wilson committee found that in 1975 there were already twenty-three holdings by insurance companies of more than 5% in 165 of the largest UK firms. In that situation, an institution cannot easily sell its share-holding when a firm runs into trouble without losing a great deal of money. It becomes more sensible to step in and try to improve the company's performance directly.*

To sum up, there is no conclusive evidence that shortage of finance is the explanation for British industry's slow growth. But while declining profitability has increased companies' need for external finance, high interest rates have made money more expensive to borrow. A tax system which encourages the diversion of savings into housing, government debt and pension and life funds instead of into direct investment in industry is not likely to encourage the lively growth of risk-taking enterprises.*

6 The price of oil: can we afford it?

'The OPEC decade' is what one might call the 1970s. They were the years when the price of oil abruptly stopped its decline which, in the 1960s, had encouraged a boom in private motoring, charter flights and badly insulated new housing. Since then, the world has withstood two massive price rises, of roughly similar magnitude in terms of their impact on economic activity. It has become clear that, at least for the 1980s, oil and its price will be the largest single barrier to prolonged international economic expansion.

This chapter looks at the implications of the two huge price rises: at how they came about, how the world coped with the first one, and what the chances are for coping with the second. The implications of the oil price rise for the world economy are peculiarly complex. They are complex partly because of the structure of the economies of some of the oil exporting countries themselves: it has been difficult for them to spend more than a part of their huge wealth on imports. But it has been complex too because it represents a large shift in the terms of trade of the oil-importing countries − in the relationship between the cost of their imports and the cost of their exports. North Sea oil in this story is not much more than a footnote, but a footnote for which we in Britain can be heartily grateful.

But first, as the Michelin Guides say, *un peu d'histoire*. The first price rise came, you may remember, in October 1973, in the wake of the surprise Yom Kippur attack by the Arabs on the Israelis. Two months later, at Christmas, the oil producers of the Persian Gulf announced a further rise which left the oil price four times the level it had been before the Arab invasion.

That blow had been about to fall for some years previously. Up to the Second World War, the market price of crude oil had been rising steadily. In the late 1940s, it fell sharply, and then stabilized through most of the 1950s. Towards the end of the 1950s, oil production began to build up: the USSR increased its output, and Libya rapidly began to exploit its reserves. Right through to the late 1960s, oil supplies grew faster than demand and the price was weak. Indeed, the main oil exporting countries formed OPEC (the Organization of Petroleum Exporting Countries) in 1960 to try to stop the price of oil from declining. They failed: the official price of Saudi Arabian oil, which was the standard by which most other crude oil prices were set, stuck at $1.80 a barrel throughout the 1960s, but was $1.30 by the beginning of the 1970s.

In the late 1960s, the closure of the Suez Canal and the tough line taken by the new revolutionary government in Libya marked the end of the buyers' market in oil. More important, the US, which was the world's largest oil producer, had become a bigger and bigger consumer of energy, particularly of oil. As the 1970s dawned, the US emerged as an increasingly important importer of oil. By 1973, the US was relying on imports for about a third of its oil. OPEC found itself supplying about 85% of world exports of oil, and thus in a powerful position to influence the prices.

Through the early years of the 1970s, a succession of events nudged the oil price up. By the summer of 1973, the price of Saudi Arabian crude oil was already at $3 a barrel. Both oil companies and oil-importing governments were already aware − and alarmed − that power was slipping away from the main consumers of oil.

For what gave the OPEC countries their market power was not the fact that they were large producers of oil, but the fact that they had a large surplus to export. The USSR, then and now, produces more barrels of oil a year than Saudi Arabia, the biggest of all the OPEC producers. Until the late 1970s, the same was true of the US. Even Britain today produces more oil than Indonesia, Kuwait, or Abu Dhabi. But the US, USSR,

73

and the UK are all large consumer of oil as well as producers. The OPEC countries are all relatively under-developed. That and their oil is about the only similarity among them. There is an inner group of Arab countries: Saudi Arabia (which accounts for about one-third of all OPEC output), Libya, Iraq, the United Arab Emirates and Qatar. They are all large producers and most have small populations. Then there are a number of non-Arab Third World countries: Iran (until the revolution the second largest producer), Algeria, Ecuador, Nigeria, Gabon, Indonesia, and Venezuela, with larger populations and smaller output.

The oil price increases of 1973 were not the end of the story, although for a few years it looked as though they might be the worst chapter. OPEC had succeeded in doing what other Third World producers of primary products had been trying to do for a long time. They had demonstrated that by unilateral action they could determine the price of their product.

But the real test of a commodity cartel is whether its participants can succeed in holding up the price of their product when demand for it declines. OPEC in 1973 had a following wind. For not only had the US emerged as a large importer of oil, putting pressure on the export market of which the OPEC countries were the main suppliers; there had also been a massive synchronized world boom in 1973. That year, production in the OECD (Organization for Economic Co-operation and Development) area of free world industrial countries had grown by a staggering 6.3%, and in most industrial countries the economy was running flat out at or above full capacity. A boom like that inevitably sucked in a tidal wave of imports, especially of primary products, and not surprisingly there were huge commodity price increases in the months before the oil price rise. The October increase was, in a sense, simply part of a wider pattern – all Third World commodity producers did very well out of the industrial world's synchronized expansion. For instance, the price of sugar and zinc rose roughly sevenfold between 1970 and mid 1974: the price of copper, lead and tin between two and three times.

But in the recession which followed the 1973 price increases and lasted through the mid 1970s, the oil price stuck at the

74

peak to which OPEC had driven it. For five years the price of oil remained largely unchanged. Indeed between the first quarter of 1974 and the end of 1978 the real price of oil — the dollar price of crude oil divided by the dollar price of world exports of manufactures — actually fell by 10%.

Then in 1979, a number of events coincided. There was an unusually cold winter. The US economy had been expanding rapidly, and the US dollar in which OPEC oil is priced had lost value sharply in 1978. And the ousting of the Shah of Iran brought oil supplies from Iran to a virtual halt. With oil companies' stocks of oil unusually low, the balance between buyers and sellers in the world oil market once again tipped in OPEC's favour. Oil companies scrambled to build up their stocks, putting more pressure on supplies. Not surprisingly oil prices rose again: the weighted average price of an OPEC barrel in 1979 was 50% higher, in nominal terms, than the average for 1978 and by the end of 1979 the real price of oil was roughly 40% above the peak to which OPEC had pushed it in 1974.*

The increases continued at a succession of OPEC meetings in 1980. At the same time, the structure of oil prices changed. Saudi Arabia, with its huge investments in the West, was anxious to pursue a more conservative policy in pricing its oil than some of the other OPEC countries. The price of Saudi Arabian crude oil became a floor price instead of a benchmark. At an OPEC meeting in Bali, Indonesia, in December, 1980 a range of official prices was set, running up to a peak of $41 a barrel for some oil — 190% above the $14 a barrel price of 1974. That was the top this time around. By the spring of 1981, a new glut of oil was beginning to undermine prices.

Although in percentage terms the second oil price rise was smaller than that of 1973, its impact on the world economy was just as large because oil prices were already at a much higher level when it took place. And there are considerable similarities between the effects of the two bouts of price rises. Each has had a number of complex implications for the world economy, which are not always easy to disentangle. Put very briefly — I will spell it out in more detail in a moment — the rise in the oil price implies a large transfer of wealth from the oil importers to the oil exporters. This transfer of wealth shows up in large

75

current account deficits run by the oil importers — and by large capital surpluses earned by the oil exporters.* Because the oil exporters cannot absorb all this additional wealth immediately, it is open to the oil importers to postpone making the transfer by borrowing some of the exporters' capital surpluses back. But this 'recycling' puts great pressure on the international financial system. Besides, the unwillingness of citizens in the oil importing countries to accept the check to their living standards which the oil price rise involves creates problems of domestic inflation. As a result, many of the oil importers respond with tough tax and monetary policies which make the inevitable deflationary impact of the oil price rise even greater than it would otherwise be.

In 1973, it was the emergence of huge current account deficits which first alarmed the industrial world. In January 1974, the 'Committee of Twenty', which had been set up by the International Monetary Fund before the oil price rise to examine the possibilities of reforming the world's monetary system, called on countries to 'accept the oil deficit'. There was considerable worry that the higher oil price would lead to a rapid spread of import controls, or to competitive devaluations. For while an individual oil importer might hope to get rid of its current account deficit by exporting more goods and services to another oil importing country, this was clearly impossible for the oil importing world as a whole. The only way for the oil importers as a group to offset the entire extra cost of oil — apart from buying much less of the stuff — would have been by a vast increase in exports to the oil exporters.*

And that, it was quite clear from the start, would not happen quickly. For most of the oil exporters were patently unable to spend their vast new revenues straight away. A few countries, Nigeria and Indonesia for instance, were so poor and so populous that they seemed likely to spend the extra money fairly fast. But even in those countries there were physical limits to the speed with which the extra wealth could be digested: projects had to be planned, port facilities improved, imports ordered, and so on. But in most of the Middle East oil exporters, the increase in revenue was so vast, the populations so small and the infrastructure of ports and roads so primitive that it seemed as though it might be many years before all the surplus revenues could be transformed into imports.

In the meantime, the oil importers as a bloc would simply have to live with this combined current account deficit. The figures were vast. But there was a potential solution in the very excess of OPEC wealth which was the cause of the oil importers' problems.

For the mirror image of the oil importers' swollen current account deficits was a swollen OPEC current account surplus. This shot from $6 billion or so in 1973 to $67 billion in 1974. This money had to be invested somewhere: and in theory, it would have been possible for the oil importers to borrow back OPEC's surplus revenues and use this capital inflow to cover their current deficits until OPEC had developed enough to buy more imports from the rest of the world.

But this raised another problem. For the internal counterpart to the impact of the oil price rise on the balance of payments of the oil importing countries was a squeeze on domestic living standards. The OPEC price rise operated very much like a large increase in excise duty on oil. A rise in the duty on oil pushes up the price of the fuel, raising the prices of all goods and services which use it and through this price rise collects revenue from the consumers who buy oil and oil-based goods and services. The OPEC price rise collected revenue in precisely the same way. But there was one crucial difference. A rise in excise duty leaves the revenue in the hands of government which may — if it chooses — offset the squeeze on consumers' living standards by reducing taxes or spending money elsewhere in the economy. But the revenue from the OPEC price rise had to be handed over to OPEC. The transfer of wealth that this involved was potentially enormous: the additional receipts of the oil exporters in 1974 were equal to nearly 2% of the total national output of the oil importing countries.

But just as it was open to the oil importers to postpone the adjustment of their current account deficits, so it was open to them to postpone the adjustment of their national living standards involved in making this massive transfer of wealth to OPEC. The mechanism was simply to borrow back OPEC's spare cash. Indeed to try to adjust straight away meant, as we have seen, simply making life worse for other oil importers and reducing the potential rate of growth for the world as a whole.

What confronted the world in 1974 was the sort of problem which Keynes had written about in Britain in the 1930s. There was suddenly a sharp increase in the level of world savings — represented by the oil exporters' unspendable revenues. The only way to maintain the level of demand was for the countries which *could* spend the money to borrow it back again.

But of course, the level of world demand was not maintained. In 1974, most governments ran restrictive tax and monetary policies which actually reinforced the contractionary effect of the oil price rise. There were perhaps three reasons for this apparent perversity.*

One was that even before the oil price rise, inflation had been accelerating at an alarming rate. A number of countries had already embarked on deflationary policies before the oil price rose. In the UK, for instance, Edward Heath's government introduced a package of tough public spending cuts early in December, before the second oil price rise took place.

Second, countries did not like the idea of getting into debt. Some of the industrial countries were particularly anxious not to run a huge and apparently timeless current account deficit. Japan, to take the most striking example, ran such tough economic policies in 1974 (partly because wages rose by 33% in the spring of that year) that the current account deficit swung from a large deficit in the first half of the year to substantial surplus in the fourth quarter.

And third, the inflationary pressures which were already troubling most governments late in 1973 were made much worse by the oil-price rise. For consumers tended to resist — more in some countries, less in others — the squeeze on their living standards which the oil price rise entailed. Even where a government was prepared to borrow back to maintain output, it was unwise to borrow back to maintain the level of personal incomes. The Labour government which took office in 1974 did just that, cutting VAT in the summer of 1974, and it reaped the whirlwind in 1976. For borrowing only postponed the need to transfer wealth to the oil exporters — it did not remove the obligation. Prudence dictated that the borrowing should be used to increase investment, either in energy conservation to reduce the size of the future transfer of wealth which would be needed, or in the production of goods and services with which OPEC's bill could eventually be met. In short, borrowing could not protect personal incomes: it merely made it possible to protect the overall level of economic growth.*

So far, I have been describing the way in which the oil price rise affected the 'real' economy after 1973; how it redistributed spending power within countries and between countries. But there was a financial counterpart to these real transfers of wealth. The vast surpluses of the oil producers − VSOP as the Treasury working party on the subject used to be called − had to be recycled from the oil exporters who wanted to invest them to the oil importers who wanted to borrow them. The exporters, it soon became clear, did not always want to invest their funds in the form in which borrowers wanted to borrow them. The exporters showed a strong preference for putting their money on deposit for short periods of time − typically three to six months − while the importers wanted to borrow to cover balance of payments deficits or investment projects which might continue for years. Some institution had to carry out the transformation: and most of the work was done and is still being done by the world's biggest banks, many of them American or British operating in the Eurocurrency market.

In the days after the oil price rises, early in 1974, there was a great deal of worry that the financial system would not be able to cope. People voiced a number of separate concerns. First, many people thought that the banks would not be able to handle the sheer volume of borrowing and lending which re-cycling would force on them. The very size of the banks, measured in terms of their capital base, would be too narrow for them to carry the load. Initially, the OPEC countries were only happy about placing deposits with a small number of very large banks. Gradually, they widened the circle.

A second and distinct worry was that the countries which needed the oil money most might find it hardest to borrow. In particular, people feared that the Third World countries might find it difficult to raise enough funds to cover their deficits. This has undoubtedly happened to some of the poorest Third World countries. But many of the others, particularly in Asia and Latin America, have survived better than was expected. This was partly because the oil price rise hit them just after a period when their own earnings from primary products had risen sharply: but also partly because some Third World countries like India and Korea have been extremely successful at exporting labour or goods to OPEC.

Third, there was a worry that the surplus funds of the oil exporters might increase the risk of financial instability. The exporters, it was argued, might suddenly decide to penalize a country by moving their funds out of its currency into others, thus wreaking havoc with exchange rates. In fact, things have worked out the other way around. The OPEC country with the largest surplus, Saudi Arabia, has played a highly conservative role both in discussions of new oil price increases and in the management of its funds. It is rather in the same position as the Prudential Assurance company on the London Stock Exchange − it cannot sell out its holding of any one currency without pushing the price against itself. But the oil exporters have found that the investments abroad are vulnerable to seizure: President Carter's decision to freeze American holdings of Iranian assets in 1980 caused deep alarm among the other oil exporters and a move away from the US dollar into European currencies.

Now the main reason why the world's financial markets were able to cope with recycling after the first oil price rise was that they did not have to cope for very long. Instead of lasting for many years, as pessimists (like me) had predicted, the oil exporters' surplus shrank with astonishing speed. In 1974, the identifiable cash surplus of the oil exporters totalled $53.2 billion. In 1978, that had dwindled to $13.4 billion. By then, even some of the Middle Eastern exporters with tiny populations and huge revenues had begun to run current account deficits.

What had happened? First, the OPEC countries had stepped up their imports much faster than most people had thought possible. In 1974 and 1975 in particular, the volume of imports grew by an average of just over 40% a year. After that, the rate of growth gradually slowed down, and it fell sharply in 1979, partly because the revolution in Iran brought home to Middle Eastern governments the risks of rapid economic development, and partly because for countries like Nigeria the money had simply begun to run out.

The second reason for the swift decline in the exporters' current account surpluses was that the rest of the world did not increase its imports of oil – and paid less for it in real terms. From 1974 until 1979, production of oil from OPEC and other Third World oil producers stuck at around 31 to 32 million barrels a day – although in 1975, at the trough of the world recession, it dropped by about 9%. One reason was that there was more oil available in the West as Alaska and the North Sea came on tap. Another was that the high price held down consumption and encouraged some effort at conservation. And third, the slow rate of world growth outside the US held down the demand for oil, which normally tends to rise in step with economic activity.

To sum up so far: the world survived the first oil price rise partly by making a larger than expected transfer of wealth to the oil exporters (the counterpart of their import boom); partly because the financial system proved more resilient than had been thought; and partly by accepting a sharp reduction in the average rate of growth and a corresponding rise in unemployment. The second oil price rise of 1979–80 may be harder to digest.

Like the price rise of 1973–4, the second oil price rise represented a deterioration in terms of trade of the OECD area of the industrial world of about 2% of its GNP.* In other words, the industrial countries were faced with the need to spend an additional amount equivalent to roughly 2% of their current output to buy the same amount of oil. The swing in OECD current balances of payments between 1978 and 1980 was roughly the same as that between 1972 and 1974 – about $1\frac{1}{2}\%$ of the area's GNP.

In some ways, the world may be better placed to sustain this new increase. Inflation is not as rampant. The first time around, the price rise burst on a world where there was no margin of spare capacity and fed rapidly through into higher wages. The second time, commodity prices were rising rather more slowly and so were unit labour costs. The pattern of balance of payments current account deficits looked like being more evenly distributed. The first time around, the US ended up with far and away the largest single counterpart of the OPEC surplus. The second time, there was not the alarming synchronization of growth rates among the industrial countries on the eve of the price rise.

The question is really whether the international capital market will once again manage to accommodate the huge volume of funds: or whether it will become essential for some new international agency to be set up to carry a share of the risk. After the first oil price rise, there was a great deal of talk about establishing a new agency — and a few half-hearted attempts. But in the end, the commercial banking system did the job.

What happens if the private banking system cannot cope this time around? Two things could go wrong. First, the world recession could be very much more severe. If oil-importing countries find that they cannot afford to borrow to cover their deficits, or if they are simply not willing to incur further commercial debt, their alternative will be to cut back activity more sharply than in the mid 1970s. A more alarming possibility is that the oil exporters might lose faith in the banking system — and decide that oil in the ground is a safer investment than cash in the bank.

The only way to escape from these worries is to reduce the dependence of the West on imported oil. That in turn means conservation and the systematic exploitation of other sources of fuel — including nuclear power. In the late 1970s, there was substantial energy saving in the industrial world. From 1960 to the early 1970s, energy use in the OECD area grew at about the same rate as its real GNP. Between 1973 and 1979, the OECD area's energy requirements rose by about 7% — real GNP over the same period increased by 17%. In 1980, the OECD area grew by 1.5%. But total energy consumption declined by 1% — while demand for oil fell 5%. The market for import oil is very much the world's residual market for energy: a relatively small improvement in energy conservation could have a substantial impact on oil imports.

There have been some striking examples of energy-saving technological development. The generation of small cars which began to roll off US production lines in the late 1970s used, on average, roughly half as much petrol per mile as the previous generation of gas guzzlers. A colour television set today consumes about a third as much electricity as its ancestors of ten years ago. Conservation will probably continue to improve over the 1980s. But it takes time, and involves large investment. Think of how long it has taken British Leyland to produce a highly fuel-efficient car in the shape of the Mini-Metro. And think of how long it will take us, as consumers, to change over our entire fleet of cars so that average fuel consumption comes down to the level the Mini-Metro can achieve. The building of houses which cost less to heat, the exploitation of new coal seams, the construction of power stations which waste less fuel, all take a long time. And in a world where demand is growing slowly and where inflation makes investment more expensive and more risky, it is not surprising that conservation has been slow.

The driving force behind conservation has been the rise in the price of oil. Between 1973 and 1979, the real price of energy to final users rose by 40%. It rose by another 15% or so in 1980. That, of course, is very much less than the rise in the price of crude oil. Indeed in several industrial countries, including Britain, real energy prices to final users in 1977 were actually well below the level of 1960.

The prices of some oil products have been protected by the unwillingness of governments to raise taxes proportionately with the rise in the oil price. As a result, the inflation-adjusted retail price of petrol actually fell in many industrial countries (including Britain but excluding the US) between 1974 and 1979. Generally speaking, industry has borne more of the rise in energy prices than the domestic consumer. And car drivers have emerged as an extremely strong political lobby throughout the West. Remember how the Liberal party defeated Denis Healey's attempt to raise the tax on petrol? Remember President Carter's unpopularity, when he wanted to de-regulate oil prices in the US?

Until conservation goes a lot further, the world can never hope to return to the growth rates of the 1960s. Each new expansion will be throttled by a new rise in energy prices. True, it looks as though the early 1980s will be another period when the price of oil declines, at any rate in real terms. That will be the result of past advances in conservation, and of the profound recession in world economic activity.

The glut of oil would not survive a new burst of growth, though. And more disturbing is the way that the West remains dependent for its continuing prosperity on the uninterrupted supply of fuel from a small and politically unstable corner of the world. Saudi Arabia deliberately helped to engineer the check to oil prices in 1981, by producing enough oil to create a glut. But there are influential voices in Saudi Arabia questioning the wisdom of continuing to deplete an irreplaceable natural resource at a rate far faster than the country's immediate financial needs can justify, and at a time when Saudi Arabia's investments are losing ground against inflation. When the West cannot preserve the value of Saudi Arabia's money, why should the Saudis continue to add to their existing pile of $150 billion of financial assets? The obvious answer to that question is too awful to contemplate.*

One final point. This chapter has hardly mentioned North Sea oil. Yet people in Britain often wonder why we should suffer from OPEC's whims when we have our own oil. In fact, we do not suffer in the same way as other countries who are not self-sufficient in oil. The price rise which they endure represents a transfer of wealth from their citizens to OPEC. We make no such transfer. When the price of oil goes up in Britain — as it does, in line with OPEC prices — the transfer which we make goes mainly to the oil companies, and what they do not keep to pay off the costs of their investments in the North Sea is passed on to the government in the form of tax revenues. So unlike Germany or Japan, Britain is not made poorer by an oil price rise.

Why should the price of our oil rise at all? It depends on whether you share Groucho Marx's view of 'Why should I care about posterity? What's posterity ever done for me?' If you do not, then you have to accept that allowing the price to rise is the best way to limit the demand for oil. Price oil cheap, and we risk the fate of the Americans, who held down the price of their domestic supplies of oil, encouraged rapid growth of lavish oil consumption (think of those monster cars of the 1950s and 1960s), and suddenly found themselves the helpless prisoners of OPEC.

84

PART TWO

Questions

1   RUNNING THE ECONOMY:
HOW MUCH DOES MONEY MATTER?

1.1 The monetarist proposition[1]

There cannot, in short, be intrinsically a more significant thing, in the economy of society, than money; except in the character of a contrivance for sparing time and labour. It is a machine for doing quickly and commodiously, what would be done, though less quickly and commodiously, without it: and like many other kinds of machinery it only exerts a distinct and independent influence of its own when it gets out of order.

John Stuart Mill, *Principles of Political Economy* (1848)

Inflation occurs when the quantity of money rises appreciably more rapidly than output, and the more rapid the rise in the quantity of money per unit of output, the greater the rate of inflation. There is probably no other proposition in economics that is as well established as this one.   Milton Friedman, *Free to Choose* (1980) p. 299

If the monetarist theory is to be a policy approach we have to know when the policy is likely to be effective. According to the

---

[1] The emphasis in the questions relating to this chapter has been deliberately placed upon the explanation of how the monetarist model of the economy is supposed to operate. We have chosen not to confuse the already complex issue by introducing evidence and analysis which casts doubts upon the validity of the model as a basis for policy decisions. Students wishing to familiarize themselves with these doubts will find *Monetarism or Prosperity* (Gould, Mills and Stewart, 1981) an excellent book which avoids the dreaded algebra.

Table 1 Money supply, inflation and output (from *Economic Trends Annual Supplement*, 1980)

		% Increase: annual rate		
		Money stock M3	Index of retail prices (Jan 1962 = 100)	GDP at factor cost—1970 prices
1971	1	12.4	8.1	1.5
	2	10.4	9.8	0.8
	3	10.4	10.1	1.5
	4	13.4	9.2	1.5
1972	1	15.0	8.0	1.4
	2	23.6	6.2	3.1
	3	25.9	6.5	2.1
	4	28.1	7.7	3.8
1973	1	26.9	8.0	8.1
	2	23.9	9.3	4.7
	3	28.1	9.2	5.1
	4	28.0	10.3	3.0
1974	1	24.9	12.9	−3.2
	2	21.5	15.9	0.4
	3	15.8	17.0	0.9
	4	—	18.2	−0.8

evidence here, when does an increase in the money supply yield an increase in inflation?

Is the same time-lag to be expected if the money supply is cut as an anti-inflationary measure?

1.2 What is money?

If the money supply is to be controlled we have to know exactly what we mean by money. Here are some possibilities in current official usage:

Retail M1: notes and coins plus sight deposits (current accounts) of the UK non-bank private sector (firms and consumers) in banks and the discount market but excluding any interest bearing deposits.

M1: Retail M1 plus any interest bearing sight deposits.

M2: M1 plus deposits of the UK public sector and time deposits of the UK non-bank private sector in banks and the discount market, but excluding Certificates of Deposit and interest bearing sight deposits.

Sterling M3: M1 plus time deposits in banks and the discount market plus Certificates of Deposit of the UK non-bank private and public sectors plus sight deposits of the UK public sector.

M3: Sterling M3 plus foreign currency deposits of UK residents in banks and the discount market.

M4: Sterling M3 plus UK non-bank private sector's holdings of Treasury bills, tax instruments and acceptance credits.

M5: M4 plus building society deposits.

Which of the above do you consider to be the appropriate measure for the money supply?

If bank deposit rates moved above building society rates to an extent that deposits moved from building society accounts into time deposits at the banks, would this affect all the money measures in the same way?

1.3 Transmission mechanism: across the exchanges

Simply because two variables appear to have moved at times in unison does not necessarily establish a cause-effect relationship between them. Monetarist theory sought to explain how a change in the money supply produces an increase or decrease in the rate of inflation. One argument described in this chapter is that the transmission mechanism operates mainly through the exchange rate. It is a view which came to be known as international monetarism and associated with a group of economists at the London Business School.

If the rate of growth of the money supply in this country is reduced, then, after a delay, output and employment fall along with money incomes. This reduction in money incomes leads to a reduction in demand, part of which would have been made on imported products. The reduction in imports leads to an appreciation of the exchange rate which, although it may affect manufacturing exports (see chapter 4) reduces the price of imports and hence weakens inflationary pressures, which helps to restore export competitiveness.

Explain how an increase in the money supply will be transmitted across the exchanges into a rise in the rate of inflation.

If monetary growth through the world increased by the same amount, would inflation be the result in all countries?

1.4 The UK framework of the money supply

From roughly 1975 onwards the government has accepted the monetarist proposition and has presumably concluded that there is a recognisable cause/effect mechanism between money supply and price level. This has led to the formulation of government economic policy with an emphasis on the control of the money supply. In particular, the relationship between the Public Sector Borrowing Requirement (PSBR) and the money supply has become of crucial importance. The analysis which follows sets out how the government has seen the control of the money supply over the past few years. Although it introduces some of the dreaded algebra referred to in the chapter, we would stress that it is not difficult and that if you follow it through step by step, monetary policy will become elementary to you. The chapter says: 'Government monetary policy tries to reduce the amount the public sector borrows to a level which is more in line with the savings which the economy generates each year. And it tries to reduce bank borrowing by the rest of the private sector.' (p. 12)

To show why governments adopt this dual approach to monetary policy you need to consider the forms in which we have money in an industrial society:

Money = bank deposits + non-bank private sector
                                 holdings of currency (cash)   (A)

As far as banks are concerned, deposits are liabilities — when they accept a customer's deposit a bank is liable to have to repay it at the customer's convenience. Banks, therefore, convert liabilities into assets, things which are worth something to them and which they can convert at some point into cash if they wish or have to. If the asset happens to yield a profit whilst the bank is holding on to it, so much the better. Assets which are easily converted into cash have the characteristic of liquidity and a portion of bank assets will always be in this form. A bank's assets are, therefore, always equal to its liabilities:

$$\text{Bank assets} = \text{bank liabilities} \qquad \text{(B)}$$

The form which a bank's financial assets will take is that of money loaned − either to the private sector of the economy or to the public sector. We can, therefore, say:

$$\text{Bank assets} = \begin{array}{l}\text{bank lending to} \\ \text{the public sector}\end{array} + \begin{array}{l}\text{bank lending to the} \\ \text{non-bank private sector}\end{array} \qquad \text{(C)}$$

The original money equation (A) can now be written substituting bank deposits with bank assets as shown in (C):

$$\text{Money} = \quad ? \quad + \quad ? \quad + \quad ? \qquad \text{(D)}$$

Before you proceed write out the expression above and then in a sentence explain what it means.

Bank lending to the non-bank private sector can be influenced by the government in a number of ways which are collectively referred to as credit policy. Interest rates can be manipulated upwards so that the demand for credit is reduced or banks can be given directives about how much they should lend or to whom they should lend (what have been called quantative and qualitative controls). But what determines the other major component of our money equation − bank lending to the public sector?

The PSBR which is covered in greater detail in chapter two is, generally speaking, the difference between government expenditure and taxation income. The government can finance this borrowing requirement either by printing notes and putting them into circulation or by borrowing from private individuals (National Savings Certificates, Premium Bonds, etc.) or by selling gilt edged securities such as Treasury Bills to the banks − who are quite happy to buy them because they represent a liquid asset. We can, therefore, say that:

PSBR = bank lending + non-bank   + non-bank
       to the public   private sector private sector
       sector   holdings of   lending to the
                       currency   public sector   (E)

The level of bank lending to the public sector, therefore, will be the extent to which the PSBR is not financed by the private sector lending money to the government or the government increasing the currency in circulation:

Bank lending to the public sector = ? − ? + ? (F)

As we are now concentrating on changes, the money equation (D) can now be written in a form showing what brings about a change in it (Δ to economists means 'the change in'). So we have:

Δ money = non-bank   + Δ bank   + Δ bank
         private sector   lending to   lending to
         holdings of   non-bank   public sector (G)
         currency   private sector

To derive the crucial expression of what determines the rate of change of the money supply in the UK, simply substitute expression (F) for 'bank lending to the public sector' in expression (G) to give:

Δ money = ? + ? + ? − ? + ?   (H)

As currency holdings are both positive (they add to the money supply) and negative (they reduce PSBR and hence the government's need to borrow from the banks) they are cancelled out leaving:

Δ money = ? + (? − ?)   (I)

The 'money' in expression (I) is the so-called Domestic Credit Expansion (DCE) equation favoured by the International Monetary Fund (IMF). The expression for an open economy is DCE plus the overseas impact on the money supply:

Δ money = DCE + overseas impact

1.5 The UK framework of the money supply

This question draws upon the analysis of the UK framework of the money supply developed in the previous section.

This model starts with one simplifying assumption: the economy is assumed to be closed. Only one country exists. This is purely because at this stage we have not considered the overseas impact on the money supply.

During the course of the year the economy experiences the following flows:

Saving	= 490	Increased currency holdings =	70
Investment	= 210	Increased bank deposits	= 280
Bank lending to		Increased holdings of	
private sector	= 210	public sector debt	= 140

a) Complete the following balance sheet showing the changes in the banking sector during the year:

   Liabilities   Assets
   Deposits   ?   Lending to the private sector   ?
                             Lending to the public sector   ?

b) Using expression (E) and the information above calculate what the PSBR for the year was.

c) Refer to expression (I) and derive a figure for DCE.

d) The DCE equation of expression (I) was derived because we wanted an accurate measure of money supply in a modern economy. Use expression (A) to verify your figure in 3.

e) What was the increase in private sector holdings of public sector debt?

1.6 Credit creation and gilt-edged securities

How is it that if a commercial bank increases its holdings of gilt-edged securities it is able to increase its lending and hence contribute to an increase in the money supply?

In the operation of commercial banks there are a multitude of ratios which govern their lending patterns. For example, banks have a ratio between their total level of demand deposits and their cash holdings and non-interest bearing deposits at the Bank of England − conventionally around 8%. There is also a ratio between the amount of loans made to consumers and the amount loaned to industrial borrowers. Banks in effect have a portfolio of lending, with each category of lending varying in its duration, degree of risk and profitability. Gilt-edged securities

91

may not be the most profitable form of lending but they are short-term, in that there is a ready market for them through the stock exchange, and as the money is loaned to government the risk element is very low.

It is claimed that if the government sells gilt-edged securities to the banks, as opposed to the non-bank private sector, it is financing its borrowing requirement in an inflationary manner. This occurs because there is a ratio between banks' lending to private sector customers and their holdings of gilt-edged securities, which represents their lending to the public sector. We will operate on the assumption that the ratio is 16.66% − if a bank has loans of £100 it will seek to hold £16.66 of government stocks. We do not ask why this is the case, we simply accept that as the banking system has developed over 400 years, codes of practice have developed with it. What concerns us is the effect of the operation of this ratio.

The following represents a simplified balance sheet of a commercial clearing bank:

Liabilities		Assets	
Deposits	£1600	Balances at Bank of England	£200
		Gilt-edged securities	£200
		Loans to customers	£1200
	£1600		£1600

The bank then uses £100 of its deposits at the Bank of England to purchase gilt-edged securities.
a) Rewrite the bank's balance sheet showing the effect of this transaction.
b) What is the ratio which now exists between gilt-edged securities and loans to customers?
c) The banking code of practice dictates that the ratio should be 16.66%. The bank can therefore increase its lending to customers until this ratio is restored. Lending creates deposits which are spending power and so the money supply increases. Re-write the bank's final balance sheet showing the increase in deposits.

1.7 Pause for thought

We used to think that you could just spend your way out of a recession and increase employment by cutting taxes and boosting government spending. I tell you, in all candor, that that option no longer exists; and that in so far as it ever did exist, it only worked by injecting bigger doses of inflation into the economy followed by higher levels of unemployment as the next step.

James Callaghan to the Labour Party Conference, September 1976

Was this suitable as an epitaph for Keynesian policies?

2 PUBLIC EXPENDITURE: HOW SHOULD IT BE CONTROLLED?

2.1 Cost-benefit analysis

to close down all those parts of the rail network which are currently highly subsidized and which carry a handful of passengers at vast expense to distant corners of the Celtic fringe.   p. 30

Consider the implications to the government of closing down the heavy loss making lines. In particular what are the implications for:
a) The subsidy given to British Rail.
b) Provision of alternative transport systems.
c) The revenue of British Rail.
d) Effects on employment.
e) Road building programmes.
f) Cost of road accidents.
g) Industrial location policy.

How much of a loss do the railways make when compared with the money the government might save from closing them down?

2.2 Privatizing the public sector

Transferring activities from the public to the private sector is one possible way for the government to reduce its expenditure. It would allow the government to cut taxes, national insurance

Table 2 National income and expenditure (from *National Income and Expenditure*, 1980, tables 9.1 and 8.1; *Economic Trends*, May 1981, p. 54)

General government expenditure	£m			
	1977	*1978*	*1979*	*1980*
libraries/museums	348	386	462	
education	7,782	8,519	9,542	
health	6,727	7,619	8,863	
total	14,857	16,524	18,867	
per head of population	£280	£300	£343	
PSBR	5,994	8,331	12,594	12,301

General government income	£m			
	1977	*1978*	*1979*	*1980*
National insurance contributions	9,495	10,107	11,538	
Rates (local authorities)	5,065	5,681	6,584	
total	14,560	15,788	18,122	
per head of population	£264	£287	£329	

contributions or rates without increasing its borrowing. It would mean that commercial organizations rather than the government would make available the services, and consumers would pay for them out of the increase in disposable income which would result from their not paying rates or national insurance contributions.

a) Do you think it would be *possible* to transfer large areas of the public sector into private ownership?
b) Are there any problems which might cause questioning of the *desirability* of such a course of action?
c) Can you suggest ways in which these problems might be overcome?

d) Go to the most recent edition of the *National Income and Expenditure (Blue Book)* and the *Economic Trends Annual Supplement* and complete the column of figures for 1980.

2.3 Pricing the public sector

Without any system of charging it is impossible to gauge how much the public really wants any particular public service.   (p. 31)

In an Institute of Economic Affairs essay published in 1976 the following was said of the rise in public expenditure:

> I must tell you quite frankly that the first reason is that people want it to happen. They ask for it to happen. Never a day goes by without my constituents writing at least half a dozen letters devising new ways of spending more public money. I think it was Enoch Powell who said 'democracy is inflationary'. My constituents constantly ask me to spend money and they do not think of it as their money and to be quite honest I do not always think of it as mine. And so it goes on being spent.
>
> John Pardoe, 'Political pressures and democratic institutions', in A. Seldon (ed.) *The Dilemmas of Government Expenditure* (1976)

a) As John Pardoe's constituents are not aware that public expenditure involves their money, use marginal utility theory to explain how their demand pattern for public sector services is perfectly rational behaviour.

b) Explain how the imposition of a charge for, for example, education would alter the demand pattern.

c) Why might this change in the pattern of demand be regarded as undesirable?

2.4 Productivity in the public sector

Productivity is a much used term but one which also suffers from lack of definition. It is very often confused with efficiency and effort. When we speak of productivity we should mean the level of production attributable to one worker (for comparative purposes we talk of production in money terms per head per period of time). We can also speak of marginal productivity — the effect on output of one extra worker; and average productivity — total output divided by the number of people who made it.

To measure productivity two things are needed: a) a defined product, the output of which can be measured; and b) a period of time in which production of the output can be assumed to be taking place. When applied to the public sector it is possible to see that productivity is not an easy concept to employ.

Consider these questions/statements and make suitable responses to them:
a) A surgeon's productivity can be measured by the number of operations he carries out in a week but the best health service is one in which no operations are necessary.
b) What is the product of a primary school — how is it to be measured?
c) If we measure the output of post delivery people as the numbers of letters delivered per hour, employees of the GPO in London will have high productivity whereas those in the rural areas of Mid-Wales will not. What does this prove?

2.5 The importance of public spending?

The philosophy that 'public expenditure is at the heart of Britain's economic difficulties' because its growth has led to a borrowing requirement which, it is argued, expands the money supply, has not gone unchallenged. Most notable of the challengers is Lord Kaldor:

This philosophy is best summarized in an oft-quoted statement of Mr Nigel Lawson, Financial Secretary of the Treasury of last January:

'Let me start with two simple facts. The first is a statistic. The PSBR is at present about $4\frac{1}{2}\%$ of total GDP — compared with an average of only $2\frac{1}{2}\%$ in the 1960s. The second is an economic relationship. That is, the PSBR and the growth of the money supply and interest rates are very closely related. Too high a PSBR requires either that the government borrow heavily from the banks — which adds directly to the money supply, or, failing this, that it borrows from individuals and institutions, but at ever-increasing rates of interest, which place an unacceptable squeeze on the private sector.'

Neither of these assertions has any empirical validity — indeed the first could hardly have been made by anyone who studies the official

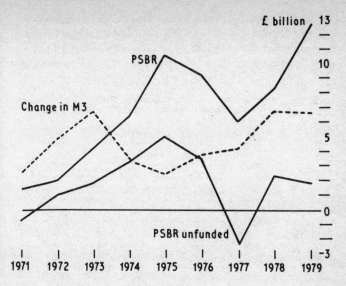

Figure 1   PSBR, the unfunded PSBR, and the change in sterling M3, annually 1971–79.

figures of the Treasury and the Bank of England, summarized in the adjoining table and graph.

The table, which contains the figures for the PSBR both 'funded' and 'unfunded' for the last six financial years, relates these to the change in the money supply, shows that the 'simple facts' are no better than fairy tales.

The part of the PSBR which, according to Mr Lawson, 'adds directly to the money supply' is that shown in column (3). For the last three financial years such 'unfunded borrowing' amounted to no more than £390m altogether while over the same period the increase in the money supply (M3) was £18.0 billion (£18,000m) or 46 times as large. Hence, the part of the PSBR financed by the banks ('by printing money' — to use Mrs Thatcher's more homely expression) could only have contributed just over 2% to the increase in the money supply since April, 1977.

Lord Nicholas Kaldor, *The Times* 6 August 1980

a) Explain what the author means by 'unfunded PSBR'.
b) If Lord Kaldor's contention is accepted, would this mean

97

Table 3 The relation of the PSBR, funded and unfunded, and changes in the money stock (from *Financial Statistics*, May 1980 (and earlier) tables 7.1, 7.2, and 7.3)

Financial years	(1) PSBR	(2) Net acquisition of public sector debt by UK non-bank private sector (funded PSBR)	(3) (1)−(2) Un-funded PSBR	(4) Changes in sterling money stock, M	(5) PSBR as % of GDP	(6) Un-funded OSBR as % of GDP	(7) Un-funded PSBR as % of the change in money stock, M3	(8) Annual growth in M2
	£m	£m	£m	£m				%H
1979−80	9,789	9,085	704	6,449	5.9 est	0.4 est	10.9	12.4
1978−9	9,282	8,537	745	5,285	6.4	0.5	14.1	11.4
1977−8	5,597	6,656	−1,059	6,233	4.3	−0.8	−17.0	15.5
1976−7	8,523	7,190	1,333	2,829	7.5	1.2	47.1	7.5
1975−6	10,585	5,320	5,265	2,453	10.8	5.4	214.6	7.0
1974−5	7,993	4,220	3,773	2,738	10.1	4.8	137.8	8.5

that the need to control public expenditure was reduced? What other reasons can be advanced for exerting careful control over the level of public spending?

2.6 Measuring public spending

The confusing way in which public expenditure has been measured in the past has allowed people to get away with statements which exaggerate the size of the public sector relative to the private sector of the economy.

Assume that public sector expenditure is entirely on wages and that we have the following figures for the economy during year 198X:

	£
Public expenditure	5000
Private sector output	5000
GDP	10,000

The public sector as a percentage of GDP is obviously 50%.

During the year private sector output in real terms grows by

5% and prices rise by 10% whilst public sector wage costs rise by 20%. At the end of the year we would have, in money terms, the following figures for the economy:

	£
Public expenditure	6000
Private sector output	5775 (real growth + money increase)
GDP	11,775

The public sector as a percentage of GDP is now 51%.

But if we measure in volume terms then the figures become:

	£
Public expenditure	5000 (volume at year 1 prices)
Private sector output	5250 (real output growth)
GDP	10,250

The public sector as a percentage of GDP is now $48\frac{3}{4}$%!

You can, therefore, prove that the public sector is either growing, or declining relatively.

This problem is made more involved because large parts of government expenditure are not counted into GDP. Transfer payments (such as unemployment benefits, student grants, etc.) will be included in the level of public expenditure but not the level of GDP.

Given the calculation:

$$\frac{\text{Public expenditure}}{\text{GDP}} \%$$

a) What happens to the size of the public sector relative to the economy as a whole when the level of unemployment rises and the rate of growth of GDP slows down? Does this say anything about the volume of resources tied up in the public sector?

b) The following table was printed in an Institute of Economic Affairs publication (*Dilemmas of Government Expenditure*, 1976), one of the many which the Institute has published to broadcast its fears about the relative size of the public sector. Tables such as this have been used to support arguments in favour of imposing expenditure cuts on the public services. What does the table really tell us?

Table 4 GNP and total government expenditure, 1960-74 (from *National Income and Expenditure* (Blue Books) 1960-74)

	1960	1965	1970	1974	1975
					Estimated
GNP £bn.	22.8	31.7	43.8	74.0	90
Index (1960 = 100)	100	140	190	325	400
Public expenditure £bn.	9.4	14.1	21.9	41.6	55
Index (1960 = 100)	100	150	230	440	580
PE as % of GNP	41.2	44.6	50	56	61
Price index (1960 = 100)	100	116	147	223	280

Increase in GNP at constant prices 1960-74   45%
Increase in PE at constant prices 1960-74   100%
Real increase in PE as proportion of GNP   36%

2.7 The importance of public spending

Explain why public spending is at the heart of economic policy, whether that policy is conducted on the lines of tight monetary control or Keynesian aggregate demand management.

3 TAXATION: WHY DO WE PAY IT?

3.1 'Over-taxed myth'

Margaret Thatcher's specific claim which arguably won her the 1979 general election was that not only was Britain 'over taxed' but we were also paying far too high a proportion of our tax liability in the form of taxes on income. This produced the basis for the 1979 budget which cut the standard rate of income tax to 30p in the pound, raised VAT to 15% and formulated the expenditure cuts which would allow the government to reduce the tax burden.

Comment upon the assertion that the over taxation argument was a myth using the figures below, which are appropriate to the time at which the argument was conducted.

100

Table 5 Proportion of total tax revenue raised in various countries by particular taxes (from Brown and Jackson, 1978, pp. 132–3)

	Income and profits	Social security contributions	Goods and services	Other	Total tax revenue – % of GDP
	%	%	%	%	%
Luxembourg	42	32	21	5	47
Holland	35	39	24	2	47
Sweden	50	19	26	5	46
Norway	41	19	38	2	45
Belgium	40	32	27	1	41½
Austria	24	30	34	12	39½
Finland	52	14	33	1	38
France	18	38	34	10	37
UK	44	18	26	12	36
Germany	36	34	28	2	35
Canada	48	8	33	11	35
Ireland	30	14	46	10	35
New Zealand	65	1	26	8	32
Italy	22	48	15	15	32
USA	44	26	17	13	30

3.2 The poverty trap

Table 6 Net weekly household* income at various earnings levels (from House of Commons Debates (Hansard, 1981) vol. 999, nos 51, 52, cols 199–208)

	£	£	£	£	£
Earnings	55	75	95	105	125
Tax	4.13	10.13	16.13	19.13	25.13
National Insurance	3.71	5.06	6.41	7.09	8.44
Take-home pay	47.16	59.81	72.46	78.78	91.43
FIS	9.50	—	—	—	—
Rent rebate	6.91	4.60	1.20	—	—
Rate rebate	2.65	1.89	0.69	0.09	—
Free school meals	2.25	2.25	—	—	—
Free welfare milk	1.30	—	—	—	—
Child benefit	9.50	9.50	9.50	9.50	9.50
Net weekly income	79.27	78.05	83.85	88.37	100.93

* This household consists of a married couple with two children aged four and six. They pay rent of £8.80, rates of £3.55 and collect Child Benefit of £9.50 (all weekly).

As the household gets successive increases in earnings it faces three marginal tax rates:

i) The explicit rate − which is the amount of the income increase that is taken away by extra tax and national insurance, expressed as a percentage of income increase.

ii) The implicit rate − which is the total loss of benefits which occurs every time earnings increase, expressed as a percentage of the income increase. And, therefore,

iii) The combined, effective marginal tax rate − which is the explicit and implicit rates added together.

a) Produce a table showing:

earnings	implicit marginal tax rate
increase in earnings	combined marginal tax rate
increased tax payments	percentage of increase in
explicit marginal tax	earnings
rate	percentage of increase in net
loss of benefits	income

b) To gain a 10% rise in net income from the starting point of £55, by how much must the household's gross earnings rise? What percentage increase in gross earnings is this?

c) If the household's gross earnings rose from £75 to £105, what percentage increase is this and what percentage increase in net income results?

Questions b) and c) should help to explain why it is irrelevant to talk about percentage wage increases in industries where there are traditionally concentrations of low-paid workers, for example local government manual workers and hospital ancillary staff.

3.3 Redistributive effects of taxation

Consider the effects of direct income tax and indirect VAT upon two 'average' households who are identical in every domestic sense except that one earns substantially more than the other.

We will consider the two extremes of taxation policy:

i) The government taxes the private sector purely through a system of direct income tax.

ii) Income tax is abolished and the private sector is taxed solely through an indirect expenditure tax.

Both families consist of a married couple with two children aged six and fourteen; they each have a mortgage of £10,000, the interest being approximately 11.75% (£1143); and life insurance premiums of £240 per annum.

a) Under this model of a direct tax system (which bears a close resemblance to the UK PAYE system circa 1978) the tax authorities grant certain allowances, namely:

	£
personal allowance	985
married man's allowance	550
children under 11	100
children 11–16	135
all mortgage interest	1143
50% of life insurance premiums	120

Thus both households gain total allowances of £3033 — they can earn up to this amount without paying any tax. On any income above £3033 (known as taxable income) they must pay 30% in tax.

The differentiating factor between the two households is that the income earner in Family A earns £5000 per annum and the income in Family B is £10,000 per annum. (It is important to realize that, at this stage, B is twice as well off as A in terms of gross income.)

Make a copy of the table below and complete the tax details for the two families:

	Family A	Family B
Earnings	?	?
Allowances	?	?
Taxable income	?	?
Tax rate	?	?
Tax paid	?	?
Take-home pay	?	?
Tax as a percentage of earnings	?	?

The tax system operates in such a way that Family B pays significantly more tax, not just as an absolute sum of money but also in terms of the proportion of income which is paid in tax. You should be able to confirm that Family B is now only 1.79 times better off than Family A.

The income tax system described here is seen to be progressive — its effects increase as income rises — 'the rich pay more'.

b) In the second tax system all consumer expenditure is taxed at 10% but personal savings are not taxed and mortgage repayments and life insurance premiums are regarded as expenditure. We further assume that Family A needs to spend all of its income whereas Family B makes savings of £3000.

Again complete the tax tables for the two families:

	Family A	Family B
Earnings	?	?
Expenditure	?	?
Savings	?	?
Tax on expenditure	10%	10%
Tax paid	?	?
Tax as a percentage of earnings	?	?

This tax system is regarded by economists as being regressive — its effect is much heavier upon lower income groups than upon high income groups.

3.4 Fiscal drag

Fiscal drag is the term used to describe how inflation increases the rate of taxation which people pay. It is fairly easy to combat using the method of taxation.

The following table illustrates the income of Mrs X who earns £5000 in her first year of work. Inflation runs at 20%, and the second column shows the effect of the lack of indexation on her tax payments.

	Year 1	Year 2 (no indexation)	Year 2 (Rooker-Wise-Lawson ammendment operating)
	£	£	£
Earnings	£5000	£6000	?
Allowances	£2000	£2000	?
Taxable income	£3000	£4000	?
Tax rate	30%	30%	30%
Tax paid	£900	£1200	?
Post tax income	£4100	£4800	?
Post tax income as a % of pre-tax income	82%	80%	?
Effective tax rate	18%	20%	?

Complete the details for year 2 showing how indexation of the tax allowance rectifies this.

The government has effectively given a sharp boost to income tax by refusing to make any change in the personal allowances which decide where tax liabilities start. There is also a crack-down on perks.

The one comfort comes on redundancy. If they lose their jobs the first £25,000 of redundancy payments will be tax free, as against the first £10,000 now.

For the last four years governments have raised the starting point for tax allowances in line with inflation – a move which ensures that it remains the same, in real terms, from one year to another.

This time the allowances should have gone up 15%, so that a married man without a mortgage would have had to start paying tax only after he had earned £2465, for instance.

The irony is that the Conservatives supported the original plans for allowances to rise automatically in line with prices and the Rooker-Wise amendment would never have reached the statute book without the Tories full backing. One of the most fervent backers for the scheme, back in 1977, was Mr Nigel Lawson, the present Financial Secretary to the Treasury.

However, the rule lays down that the Chancellor need not raise the allowances to match inflation if he has the support of the House.

Sir Geoffrey claimed in his speech that indexation was out of the question — for it would cost the Treasury some £2500 million in a full financial year.

Tom Tickell and Rod Chapman, *The Guardian*, 11 March 1981

Explain the phrase 'for it would cost the Treasury some £2500 million in a full financial year'.

3.6 The incidence of indirect taxation

Consider the following information concerning the demand and supply schedules faced by a particular firm engaged in the production of whisky.

Price pence	Quantity supplied thousands per week	Quantity demanded thousands per week
200	—	80
300	—	76
400	20	—
450	40	—
500	70	—
550	90	—
600	110	65
700	—	61
1000	—	40

Construct axes, with the price axis ranging from 0–1000p and the quantity axis ranging from 0–130. Plot the co-ordinates given above and from them produce supply and demand curves. This information will combine to give you the market price.

The government now introduces a specific tax of £1 per bottle and Customs and Excise men visit the factory and monitor the level of production. The firm must now pay to the government £1 for every bottle sold which means that if it sells whisky for £5 a bottle it will only receive £4. (Selling price — tax = revenue to the firm.) According to the supply schedule above, if the firm receives only £4 per bottle it is only willing to supply 20,000. If the old price had been £6, then after it has paid the tax to the government the firm receives £5, at which price the supply figures tell us it will offer 70,000 to the market. You can now construct on the same axes, a 'post tax' supply curve because we have the following information:

106

	Before duty			After duty	
Price	Money received	Quantity in thousands	Money received	Price
£5	£5	70	£5	£6
£6	£6	110	£6	£7

You can interpret this information in either of two ways:
i) To supply the same amount (70,000) the firm wants more money.
ii) For a given price (£6) the firm will supply less (110,000−70,000).

The after tax supply schedule can now be translated into a new supply curve and the new market price is derived.

Now answer the following questions:
a) What has the firm's response been to the introduction of the duty?
b) Why did the firm not just pass on the entire tax increase to the consumer?
c) It appears that 20p has gone missing and yet we know the government will collect its £1 — where will the 20p come from?

Now repeat the analysis using exactly the same supply schedule and an identical introduction of duty but with the following market demand pattern:

Price in pence	Quantity demanded in thousands
400	110
450	90
500	69
550	40
600	20

Explain what the difference is between the second outcome and the first. Why was the behaviour of the firm so different?

3.7 The incidence of income tax

What are the arguments put forward to support the view that the true incidence of income tax falls upon initiative and effort?

3.8 Tax and distribution

Whatever form the taxation may take, it is paid to finance the public sector which has grown substantially in recent years. People do not pay taxes on an equal basis but neither do they use public sector services to an identical extent. We must consider also that if the public sector did not provide the services, then people would have to buy them.

Consider the following cases:

Person A is married with three children, two of whom are in a comprehensive school and one is about to go to university. The family live in a council house and between them they pay about £500 in taxes per annum.

Person B is single and runs a classy fashion boutique. She lives in a luxury flat and estimates that her annual tax contribution is £5000 per annum.

Explain what would happen if overnight the public sector provision of services was abolished, together with all forms of taxation. As you consider the two cases above explain what is meant by 'tax and transfer'.

3.9 Negative income tax

In this system of negative income tax all social security payments and benefits have been replaced by a single payment, the size of which depends upon the circumstances of the household concerned. All personal tax allowances have been abandoned and income tax is imposed on all income except the social dividend which, therefore, acts as a minimum wage. Figure 2 shows how the system would operate: OB is the no-tax line along which gross income = net income; OA is the social dividend. As income rises from zero, the extra earned income above the social dividend is taxed so that net income A—O rises less quickly than

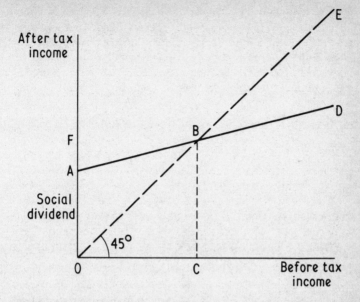

Figure 2   Negative income tax system

gross income O−E. Income level OC is the break even point −
below it people have an income above that which they receive
from employment, and they are in receipt of some social
dividend. Above C, although income always continues to rise,
income after tax is less than income from employment − people
are contributing to the social dividend.

a) When triangle OAB = triangle BED, what is happening to
   the system?
b) Where is the 'poverty trap' in this system?
c) If we raise the social minimum income to OF and leave the
   break even point at B what problem have we now built into
   the system?

3.10   Negative income tax, or benefits in kind

A negative income tax of the social dividend type has to be
assessed in terms of its efficiency in achieving the goals set by the

government for it. If we assume i) that the aim is to ensure that all members of the population are guaranteed the minimum essentials of life; and ii) the government wishes to spend as little as possible in achieving i), then we can observe the difference between employing a system of negative income tax, or a system of benefits in kind (free housing, school meals, medical care, etc.).

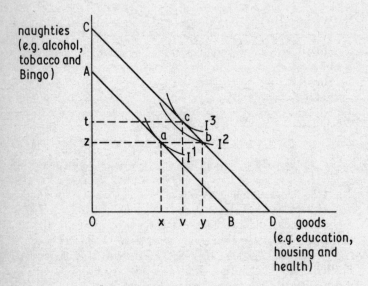

Figure 3   Negative income tax

The household starts at point 'a' consuming Ox of 'goods' and Oz of 'naughties'. The government decides that Ox is below the minimum of goods which people should consume and so it introduces a benefit in kind system and gives the household some extra goods. The household cannot choose what form the benefits should take — they are given what it is thought will be good for them — but they can, of course, not take the benefits if they so choose.

This results in a movement from a–b where the household still consumes Oz of naughties but is now consuming Oy of goods.

110

a) Using indifference analysis explain how the household feels about its new consumption combination.

If the government decided to opt for the cash payment of benefit involved in a negative income tax system then households receive an increase in income which shifts the budget constraint line outwards from AB to CD and puts the household in equilibrium at c.

b) What is the household's consumption pattern at c?
c) What has the household done with the benefit income?
d) How does the household feel about point c relative to point b?
e) How is the government likely to feel about where the money has gone?
f) Not everyone sees a 'good' as a 'good' — what relevance does this piece of philosophy have to the alleviation of poverty?

4 DE-INDUSTRIALIZATION: HAVE THE JOBS GONE FOR EVER?

4.1 Public sector employment growth

Consider for a moment the industries which have grown rapidly in the public sector over the past thirty years.
a) What are the growth jobs which have been taken increasingly by women?
b) Why are these jobs regarded as being almost exclusively for women?
c) Would it help if these jobs were seen as being available to both men and women?

4.2 Selling services abroad (diversifying the industrial base)

Just how realistic is it to consider a change in the industrial base of the country which results in service industries replacing manufacturing industries as foreign currency earners and employers? Consider the substitution of car exports for overseas tourists – both count as foreign currency earners.

Exporting a Mini-Metro to Germany will bring in £4000 of foreign currency earnings whilst a reasonably priced hotel will charge foreign tourists £150 for a week's full board (outside London), and each tourist can be assumed to spend a further £100 per week on other purchases. In this case, therefore, for every car not exported we need to attract an extra sixteen foreign tourists.

Table 7 Overseas travel and tourism (from *Tourism Policy and International Tourism in OECD Member Countries*, OECD 1980, pp. 132, 151)

Tourist receipts for the UK 1978–9		
1978	*1979*	*%*
£2,507.3m	£2,764.9m	+10.3

Number of visits completed by overseas visitors to the UK 1979	
Qtr 1	1,855,000
2	3,240,000
3	4,951,000
4	2,454,000
Total	12,499,000

Table 8 Number of passenger cars exported from the UK 1979–81 (from *Economic Trends* no. 331, May 1981, p. 132)

Quarter	*1979*	*1980*	*1981*
	thousands		
1	37.6	35.9	23.1
2	34.9	33.1	—
3	26.0	29.5	—
4	32.4	18.1	—

a) If every car was worth £4000 and every tourist spent £250, how many tourists would we need to compensate for the foreign exchange earnings loss if we stopped exporting cars?

b) What growth rate in the tourist industry would that represent?

c) Would there be any further balance of payments effect or are car exports and tourist exports perfectly interchangeable in this respect?

d) Explain why tourism is likely to be a more labour intensive employer than manufacturing.

e) Without going to the extreme of stopping our exports of cars completely we could make a partial substitution of tourism (services) for cars (manufacturing) as a foreign exchange earner — would such a policy be possible/desirable and how could the government seek to promote this structural change in the economy?

But there is a wider problem isn't there? The assumption used to be that unemployment would be a disagreeable but temporary consequence of the application of monetary policy. But now it's a world-wide phenomenon and it looks as though we are going to have to live with unemployment on a higher level than anyone has been used to. How do we come to terms with that?

Well, you would have a larger proportion of your national income going to services. Tourism is one of them. Look at the number of jobs it's created — in the aircraft industry, in chartered flights, in hotels, in holidays. Transport is a service industry. Insurance is a service industry. So is banking. They go world-wide.

Leisure itself is a service industry. It is part of your gross domestic product. So yes, I think that we shall probably have a smaller proportion of our people in manufacturing but a bigger proportion in services.   *The Sunday Times*, 3 May 1981

Above is an extract from an interview by Ronald Butt, printed in *The Sunday Times*. Who do you think is being interviewed? You can decide for yourself whether or not you think this adds weight to the argument.

4.3 Crowding out

The elementary version of the Bacon and Eltis crowding out

argument was not new but rather a re-statement of what had been referred to as the 'Treasury view'.

At this time the widespread existence of unemployed workers and immense surplus stocks of coal above ground and other raw materials, were apparent for all to see. In the circumstances of his time he (Keynes) suggested that the government, rather than run a financial surplus or seek to balance its budget, should in fact be prepared to run a deficit, a proposal against all the canons of sound finance, as supported by traditional neo-classical economic doctrines. Indeed in 1929 the British Treasury had published a refutation of policies then advocated by the former Liberal prime minister, Lloyd George, that the Treasury should be prepared to run a financial deficit to create a sufficient demand to mop up persistent unemployment. In their view any demand created in this way, by expenditure on new public works, roads, buildings, etc. would simply be at the expense of real resources which should be going into the private sector. Their answer to the unemployment problems of the economy was to let wages and other costs eventually move down to their natural level so that Say's law could in the longer run, once again begin to work. Unfortunately as Keynes provocatively pointed out 'in the long run we are all dead'.

John Hutton, *The Mystery of Wealth* (1978) p. 121

a) What is meant by 'traditional neo-classical doctrines'?
b) What does Say's law state?
c) In the 1920s the consequence of the Treasury view was un-employment — what did Bacon and Eltis claim was the consequence of reversing the Treasury view?
d) What did Keynes mean by 'in the long run we are all dead'.
e) Explain how it can be argued that the 1979 election resurrected the Treasury view.

4.4 Stages of economic growth

In 1959 W. W. Rostow wrote a book entitled *Stages of Economic Growth*. In it he suggested that all economies pass through a series of phases as they develop from fairly poor agri-cultural societies to highly industrialized, mass consumption economies. The five stages he identified were:
 i) The traditional society.
 ii) The transition phase — when the traditional social and economic values are challenged.

114

iii) 'Take off stage' — when the traditional values have been overcome and economic growth becomes a normal condition.
iv) 'Drive to maturity' — the economy diversifies its industrial base, adopts new technology and enters more into international trade.
 v) The age of mass consumption — when there is an affluent population and the leading sectors of production are durable and sophisticated consumers' goods and services.

Not everyone accepts Rostow's view of economic development but it is interesting to reflect upon the following points:
a) Do you think the UK is still in the 'drive to maturity' or have we arrived at the age of mass consumption?
b) It is possible that Rostow failed to recognize a sixth stage which some commentators refer to as the 'post industrial state'. What sort of an economy do you think that might be?

4.5 Crowding out

The 'present government's economic policies' referred to here are those aimed at cutting back the non-market sector and, therefore, reducing the public sector demand for workers (that is, create unemployment in the public sector).

a) If the Bacon and Eltis logic is correct what should follow?
b) What type of evidence would you want to see as a result of the government's policies which would indicate whether or not the predictions of the 'crowding out' theory were accurate?

4.6 'Privatizing' the public sector

Studies by the Institute of Economic Affairs (*Over-ruled on Welfare*, 1979) indicate that there is a demand for education — people are prepared to consider paying in order to acquire the education they regard as necessary. The public concern over the cuts in the education service over the past ten years indicates that people are reluctant to see the education service decline. We might interpret this as people wanting more education and being willing to pay for it. Yet Mrs Thatcher's government cut back the state education system, primarily (although there are other reasons) because it needed, according to its economic philosophy, to reduce its borrowing requirement and the level of taxation. Thus education is prevented from becoming the employer it could be if the demands of the public were met. Possibly if education were privatized it might expand as an employer. But what does it mean to privatize education? This debate normally becomes clouded with the intricacies of voucher systems, and so on. Consider, however, the following statements:

i) 'Schools are not occupied for 25% of the year at all'.
ii) 'For 28% of each week schools are empty'.
iii) 'Schools are used for about ten hours of most days when they are open'.
iv) 'Schools are equipped with sports and leisure facilities, dining and catering facilities, conference and theatre facilities as well as extensive teaching facilities'.

a) What if the government 'gave' schools to teaching staff for the time outside that used for statutory education (of 5–16 year olds)? What could be done with the facilities? Could schools earn money and what could they do with it? Would this expand the employment potential of education?
b) Do you think education could ever become a large scale exporter?

4.7 Crowding out: formal analysis

The 'subtle' version of crowding out can be explained using national income identities.

1 *Output = Expenditure*. There is no point in production unless you can sell, so output will tend to adjust to the level of demand (expenditure).
2 *Expenditure = C + I + G + (X−M)*. The level of demand in an economy comes from four sources − consumers (C); firms, for purposes of investment (new factories, etc.) (I); the public sector (Government − G); and exports (X). But part of each of these is spent on imports (M) and this is subtracted. Thus we are left with the expenditure figure which domestic

firms experience − it is the employment generating level of demand.

3 So *Output = C + I + G + (X − M)*. The level of output (GNP) of an economy goes to satisfy the demands of consumers, firms, government and overseas demand, less the amount of each of them which is met from imports.

4 Therefore *(X − M) = Output − (C + I + G)*. The balance of payments is determined by how much of the domestic output is left over after domestic demand has been satisfied. If one of the elements of domestic demand increases then three things are possible:

  i) either output increases to meet the rise in demand;

 ii) one of the other elements of demand is reduced to make goods available to meet the increase; or

iii) the extra demand is satisfied by imports.

Simulation 1

Output = 100 Consumer expenditure = 55 Exports   = ?
Imports = 15   Investment   = 20 Government = 10
What is the balance of payments position?

Simulation 2

Output = 100 Consumer expenditure = 55 Exports   = ?
Imports = 15   Investment   = ?   Government = 20
As a consequence of the increase in government expenditure what must happen either to the balance of payments, or the level of investment?

The natural growth rate of the economy is 2.6%. What difference does it make if that output expands over the year?

Simulation 3 (using the original values in simulation 1)

Output = 100 Consumer expenditure = ?   Exports   = 15
Imports = 15   Investment   = 20 Government = 20
As the government increases its expenditure on the public sector, it also raises income tax to finance the expenditure. This results in a fall in personal disposable income which governs the level of consumer expenditure. What happens to consumer expenditure?

Simulation 4

This fall in personal disposable income and the ability to buy goods and services represents a fall in living standards to workers, who are not prepared to regard the extra public sector services as offsetting this fall. Organized labour therefore fights back and gains pay increases to compensate for the tax increases and can therefore maintain its level of consumption. Output, however, is spoken for, so what possible effects might these events produce?

Output = 100   Consumer expenditure = 55   Exports   = ?
Imports = ?   Investment   = ?   Government = 20

4.8 Factor mobility

If the service sector of the economy were to grow in relation to the manufacturing sector and the shedding of labour from manufacturing continued unabated, then there should be a transfer of resources from manufacturing to services. How is this transfer to be effected?

a) One line of thought is that given a reduction in demand for labour of one kind and increase in demand for it of another, the labour markets will naturally effect the transfer. Explain how this will operate, possibly with the aid of diagrams.

b) Explain why it might be difficult for ex-car factory workers to become couriers − what problems might they experience and what is needed if the transfer is to be effected?

4.9 Loss of competitiveness: foreign exchange market

The market for foreign exchange is no different from any other market. Exchange rates are simply prices of currencies in terms of another currency. As prices, exchange rates are subject to the forces of supply and demand. If the demand for sterling increases then, with the supply held constant, it will rise in price (i.e. whereas previously US$1 got you £1, it now gets 50p) Equally if the supply of sterling is increased, the pound falls in value in terms of other currencies. In analysing exchange rate changes all you have to do is to consider any action affecting sterling in terms of 'does it increase or reduce the supply or demand of sterling to the foreign exchange markets?'

Draw the following table and tick the options which you consider to be the most likely in each case:

Action	Effect: Increases the supply of £	Reduces the demand for £	Increases the demand for £	Reduces the supply of £	Revalues £	Devalues £
Rise in imports into UK						
Fall in exports from UK						
UK interest rates lower than other OECD countries						
Fall in imports into UK						
Rise in exports from UK						
UK interest rates higher than other OECD countries						

4.10 Loss of competitiveness: exchange rates and trade flows

If the domestic UK price of a product is £100 and the exchange rate is $1.80 = £1, how much will the same product sell for in the US?

If domestic inflation in the UK raises prices by 10% whilst there is no inflation in the US, how much will the product sell for in the US, assuming the authorities in the UK act to hold the exchange rate constant at $1.80?

What is it reasonable to assume will happen to UK exports? If this does happen what can we say about the nature of the demand pattern for UK exports?

If US demand for UK products falls, will the demand for sterling, with which to pay for them fall also? What effect will this have upon the exchange rate?

If inflation raises UK prices by 10% and as a result, the exchange depreciates to $1.64 = £1, how much will the UK product cost in the US now?

To conclude, allowing the exchange rate to depreciate can offset the effects of inflation in export prices — it can preserve competitiveness.

But at what cost? What effect does a depreciation of the exchange rate have upon import prices?

4.11 Loss of competitiveness: interest rates

Consider the case of a multi-national corporation which wishes to leave $10 million on deposit with a bank but has no preference for any particular bank or country but simply seeks the highest rate of return on its deposit. At the outset the money is deposited in New York, earning 8% and then interest rates in London move to $12\frac{1}{2}$%. It obviously pays the multi-national corporation to shift its deposit to London. If it switches dollars for sterling through the foreign exchanges, what will this do to the exchange rate and UK export prices?

4.12 Loss of competitiveness: North Sea oil

At the moment the UK imports about 50% of its food requirement — as an importer this leads to a supply of sterling to the foreign exchange market. What would happen if we gradually became self-sufficient in food? The supply of sterling would be reduced. So what would be the effect upon the exchange rate and export prices?

At the CBI's annual conference on 10 November 1980 Sir Michael Edwardes, Chairman of British Leyland said of North Sea oil: 'If they [the government] can't find a way of living with North Sea oil I say leave the bloody stuff in the ground.'

Explain why he should have felt this way at that particular time.

4.13 The CEPG case for import control

The first stage of the argument is the claim that industry is only likely to be competitive when the economy is going through a period of growth.

Table 9 Average annual percentage increase in GDP and output per person per hour (OPPH) in manufacturing 1963–79 (from Gould, Mills and Stewart, 1981)

	1963–73		1973–6		1976–9	
	GDP	OPPH	GDP	OPPH	GDP	OPPH
Japan	10.2	11.2	2.5	2.0	5.8	7.7
France	5.5	6.7	2.8	3.9	3.2	3.9
Italy	4.7	7.0	2.1	2.3	2.8	3.0
UK	3.3	4.5	0.4	1.3	1.3	1.2

a) Explain why productivity is more likely to increase when the economy is expanding than when it is contracting.

b) Conventional demand management policies might seek to achieve the growth required by the level of government expenditure. If the government were to raise its expenditure by £1000m what effect would this have upon GNP if the following conditions applied to the economy:

marginal propensity to import = 0.2 (one fifth of any increase in demand will go on imported products)

marginal propensity to consume = 0.6

What will happen to the balance of payments as the economy expands?

c) The object of import controls can be seen as making the marginal propensity to import equal to zero. Explain what this means.

4.14 Import controls

A country's sole import consist of 1000 units of a product at a price of £2 each. The government seeks to cut the import bill by 33% at a time when elasticity of demand for imports is thought to be in the region of 1.5 and the rate of exchange is £1 = $3.

a) What is the initial sterling import bill?

b) Which of the following policies is likely to be most effective in terms of cutting the import bill:

i) a devaluation of the pound by 30%;

     ii) an import quota reducing the volume of imports by 30%;

     iii) a tariff on imports increasing their price by 30%?

c) If the demand for imports is reduced what can we assume will happen to the demand for and price of domestic products?

d) What are the likely consequences for exports following the introduction of policies i), ii), or iii)?

4.15 Import controls: Third World countries

The following is an extract from an article by Iain Guest in *The Guardian*, 20 May 1981 about the renewal of the Textile Multi-Fibre Arrangement (MFA), which is operated by the EEC against imports from outside the community.

Given the desperate state of the textile industry both in Europe and Britain (which lost 166,000 jobs between 1970 and 1975) there is at first sight an inescapable logic to an arrangement that imposes quotas on imports of clothing and textiles from twenty-six low-cost Third World countries. . . . That said, however, where exactly does the threat to Europe's textiles come from? In fact, the industry is far from on its last legs. In 1979 Europe registered a healthy surplus in trade with other industrialized trading partners − of over $5 billion. Two years ago a deputy chairman of ICI observed, at a seminar in London, that even Britain's ailing textile industry was developing technically as fast as aerospace − Concordes and all. But it is precisely this change from dark satanic and old labour-intensive looms that is costing jobs. Between 1970 and 1975, new technology cost 143,000 jobs in the British textile industry, and the process has been speeded up by rapid concentration. (According to one UNCTAD study Courtaulds, Carrington Viyella and Tootal between them account for 70% of all spindle hours, 50% of loom hours and one half of the total employment in finishings.)

Imports by contrast are estimated to have cost 85,000 jobs between 1970 and 1975. But the bulk of these will have come from other developed countries whose trade is not subject to any rigorous MFA. Between 1979 and 1979 while Hong Kong's exports to Europe fell from 144.6m tons to 134.9m, the US's increased from 150.7m to 211.5 millions.

Not only does Hong Kong depend on textile − over 40% of the colony's workforce is employed in the industry − but, as the delegate from Hong Kong bitterly pointed out in Geneva two weeks ago, Hong Kong does not have a protected home market or subsidize its industries.

The US by contrast achieved a mighty boost for man-made fibres by subsidized oil and the falling dollar.

Iain Guest, *The Guardian*, 20 May 1981

a) How has the US supported its textile industry?
b) What is 'sweated labour' and explain how imposing import tariffs on textile goods is likely to encourage practices in Third World countries which were outlawed here nearly a century ago.
c) Why is the MFA enforced against countries like Hong Kong but not against the US?
d) The Brandt Report has argued that the future development of Third World countries should concentrate on labour-intensive industries in which they enjoy a comparative advantage. Which is in the best interest of the European nations − the Brandt Report or the MFA?

5 THE CITY: HAS IT FAILED BRITISH INDUSTRY?

5.1 Interest rates

a) If at the beginning of a year, during which inflation turns out to be 15%, you deposit £1000 in a building society offering a rate of interest of 10%, how much better off are you at the end of the year?
b) If you think that you would be better off you are suffering from a disease which economists refer to as 'money illusion' and you are welcome in all banks and building societies.

If at the start of the year you had bought £1000 of jewellery and prices rose by 15%, how much is your jewellery worth? If you lost the jewellery, therefore, how much would it cost to replace? So how much better off were you before you lost the jewellery?
c) If you know that the rate of inflation is going to be 10% next year and you think that 5% is a fair return on your savings, what rate of interest will you ask for from a bank/building society?

d) Consider and comment on the following statement: 'If inflation is 10% and I save £1000 with a building society at an
interest rate of 5% and they then lend to a house buyer at a
rate of 10%, I am volunteering to pay the interest on his/her
mortgage.'

5.2 Savings pattern in the UK

The evidence regarding consumer behaviour for the period
1968–80 is as follows:

Table 10 Consumer behaviour (from *Economic Trends Annual
Supplement*, 1981, pp. 20, 114)

Year	Total personal disposable income £	Consumers' expenditure £	Personal savings ratio	Consumption ratio	Retail Price Index (1975 = 100)
1968	29,782	27,528	7.6	92.4	48.4
1969	31,793	29,233	8.1	91.9	51.0
1970	35,018	31,778	9.3	90.7	54.2
1971	38,531	35,599	7.6	92.4	59.3
1972	44,507	40,183	9.7	90.3	63.6
1973	51,798	45,759	11.7	88.3	69.4
1974	60,694	52,489	13.5	86.5	80.5
1975	73,768	64,424	12.7	87.3	100.0
1976	84,768	74,751	11.8	88.2	116.5
1977	95,483	85,474	10.5	89.5	135.0
1978	112,303	98,395	12.4	87.6	146.2
1979	133,153	114,805	13.8	86.2	165.8
1980					

a) Personal savings ratio is the percentage of disposable income
which is saved and consumption ratio is the percentage
which is consumed. What are these two measures conventionally known as in economic theory?
b) What do you notice about the combined value of the
Personal savings ratio and Consumption ratio? Can you
explain why this value occurs?
c) If we express the change in the level of consumption for each

of the years as a percentage of the change in total personal disposable income, what have we measured?

d) Work out the amount of savings made by the personal sector in each of the years and verify that the figures confirm the statements in chapter five concerning the relationship between personal savings and GDP. (GDP in 1968 = £43,468m)

5.3 'An investment as safe as houses'

The following passage seeks to explain in detail why housing and building societies attract a large proportion of personal sector saving.

A man buys a £20,000 house with a 25-year mortgage of £18,000 and a £2000 deposit. House prices rise with inflation, say at 10% a year (in the seven years to 1978, inflation averaged 14%, but house prices rose by 18% annually on average). The building society's lending rate is 12% (in fact it has averaged 10.5% even in the past seven years of raging inflation). This is reduced by tax relief to 8% (or much less for a higher-rate tax payer). After seven years, the house is worth £39,000, the outstanding mortgage debt is £16,000 and so the owner's equity has multiplied elevenfold from £2000 to £23,000. Of course, retail prices generally have roughly doubled too. So, in real terms, the £2000 deposit has grown to £12,000. Thus annual payments of £1600 in interest (after tax relief) and capital have produced a rate of return of 16%, tax free. After inflation, this is still a handsome 6% per year.

But things are really better than that. The mortgage payments have also been providing a place to live, saving money that would otherwise have been spent on rent. If an annual rent of £1000 is imputed for the cost of renting a similar home – and where can one rent a £20,000 house for a rent of less than £20 a week, fixed for seven years? – the rate of return soars to an incredible 28% per annum, still of course tax free. There is probably no business anywhere in the world that is a better hedge against a vicious tax system than being a home-owner in Britain. It is hardly surprising that in 1976, 41% of Britain's personal wealth was tied up in housing, compared with just 20% in 1960.

The Economist, 24 March 1979

a) The National Income and Expenditure Blue Book speaks of 'an imputed income is included for owner-occupied dwellings and farm-houses.' Explain what this means.

b) If the government wanted to divert savings away from 'dwellings' and chose to do this by making house purchase less attractive, suggest a number of ways in which the tax system might be adjusted to achieve this.

c) It is frequently argued that as council owned housing estates are characterized by new cars, caravans, etc., it is quite obvious that the tenants should not be charged subsidized rents as they can clearly afford more. They are 'a drain on the tax payer'. Property owning economists with mortgages would do well to avoid this argument. Why?

5.4 Equity prices

Because a second-hand market exists for equities, the price at which they are sold can vary as the supply of a particular share to the market varies or if the demand for it changes. If a large group of shareholders in Barclays Bank are persuaded by the anti-apartheid movement to sell their shares and demand remains constant, we would expect the price to fall — but why is it that share prices suddenly move about together?

One way to answer this is to imagine that you have bought a share in ICI for which you paid £3 and that at the end of the year the company announce that the tax paid dividend per share will be 30p, representing a 10% return on your share. If you could have got 11% by lending your money to a local authority for two years you might regard the return somewhat unenthusiastically.

But then a number of highly respected 'City analysts and editors' make predictions that ICI's profits are going to get better.

a) If by chance the pundits are right and ICI pay a 45p dividend per share next year, what would your rate of return be for that year?

b) If you decided to buy more shares on the assumption that the dividend would remain at 45p and the bank deposit rate at 10%, how much would you be willing to pay for each share?

c) Seven out of ten economic forecasters predict an imminent fall in the rate of interest to 8%. By how much might you expect your ICI share to rise in price?

5.5 Personal sector savings

The chart below is from the Treasury's Economic Progress Report[1] No. 130, February 1981. In what way could it be said to illustrate the reasons for Britain's poor economic growth record during the 1970s?

Table 11   Sources and uses of personal sector capital funds in 1979

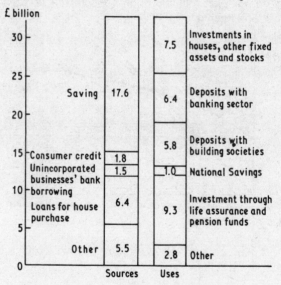

5.6 Savings behaviour: economic theory

The conventional economic wisdom regarding the relationship

[1]   The Economic Progress Report is the Treasury's monthly report to the nation on the general state of the economy. It also contains specific articles on areas of particular concern. Although they tend to employ Whitehall jargon and understatement the articles are fairly easy to read and they have the advantage of being free! To obtain a regular copy, write to: PDSD Distribution Unit, Central Office of Information, Hercules Road, London SE1 7DU.

between the rate of saving and the rate of price increases is best summarized in the following passage:

If households expect an inflation to occur, they may be willing to purchase durable goods they would otherwise not have bought for another one or two years. In such circumstances purchases made now yield a saving over purchases made in the future. By the same argument, an expected deflation may lead to postponing purchases of durables in hopes of purchasing them later at a lower price.

(Lipsey, 1975, p. 518)

a) Using the income and expenditure model shown in figure 4, indicate the changes which Lipsey predicts will occur if inflation is anticipated.

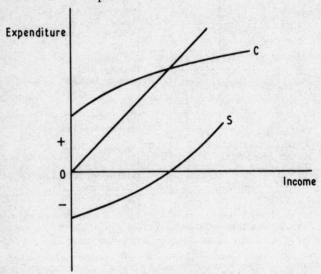

Figure 4

b) In what way can we say that this is a further example in economics of self-fulfilling expectations?

5.7 Ownership of companies

As I have just noted, as the corporation gets larger, its decisions become more complex. That reduces the power of uninformed outsiders and particularly of the stockholders. . . . No owner large or small who is not part of the technostructure has access to the information that allows of useful judgement on decisions. No persons who is not intimately involved with the everyday exchange of information in General Motors can be useful on a decision on a major new automobile design or whether to open a plant in Singapore or Taiwan. No stockholder in Shell can say anything helpful on tactics for dealing with Arab states especially since most of those dealings are not even revealed to any stockholders at least until they are completed.

> (Galbraith and Salinger, 1981, pp. 69–70)

Ownership of shares in the UK is becoming concentrated in the hands of the financial institutions. In the light of this and the above comment from Galbraith and Salinger, what are the arguments for and against companies being controlled by:

a) small private shareholders;
b) the management;
c) representatives of financial institutions who have major investments in the company;
d) the company's bankers;
e) the work force?

5.8 Taxing dividends

A tax system which encourages the diversion of savings into housing, government debt and pension and life funds, instead of into direct investment in industry. (p. 71)

How does the tax system operate to influence the flow of savings in this way? The tax system used in this example is a model of the UK tax system except that for ease of calculation the following tax rates are assumed: Income tax standard rate $= 33.33\%$, Corporation tax $= 50\%$.

Consider a very simple situation in which an individual who pays tax at the standard rate wishes to place £2000 of savings and the choice open is either to put it in a building society share account, or to buy shares in a local manufacturing company. Assume that the latter course of action is taken and that at the end of the year the company allocates pre-tax profits to this shareholder of £200.

129

a) What rate of return on the shareholding does this represent?

Corporation tax, however, is levied on the profits of the company and part of this tax payment is a pre-tax payment of income tax at the standard rate. The shareholder receives the dividend 'tax paid': in other words, after the company has deducted tax at basic rate and handed the proceeds to the Inland Revenue. So the saver in question will receive a dividend cheque for £100 and a tax paid certificate for £50 − the missing £50 has of course gone to the government as corporation tax.

b) What rate of return on the £2000 shareholding does the dividend cheque represent?

The table below shows the rates of interest paid by a leading building society over the past nine years. This rate of interest is also one which tax has been prepaid at a standard rate. In recent years, with interest rates persisting in double figures, the opportunity cost of holding ordinary shares has been very high, even before one considers the administrative commissions associated with buying them.

Table 12 Building Societies Association's recommended interest rates on ordinary shares 1973−81 (from *Building Societies in 1980*, Building Societies Association 1981, table A2)

Recommended	*new rate*
effective date	%
1973, 1 October	7.50
1975, 1 June	7.00
1976, 1 May	6.50
1976, 1 November	7.80
1977, 1 May	7.00
1977, 1 July	6.70
1977, 1 November	6.00
1978, 1 February	5.50
1 July	6.70
1 December	8.00
1979, 1 August	8.75
1 December	10.50
1981, 1 January	9.25
1 April	8.50

Pension funds do not have to pay income tax − they are treated rather like charities. If a pension fund purchased the same block of shares in the same manufacturing company, it would receive the dividend cheque and the certificate of tax paid, but by presenting the latter to the Inland Revenue it could claim a tax refund of £50.

c) What is the rate of return to the pension fund on the share-holding?

As long as the administrative costs of the pension fund are no greater than the costs of brokerage on share purchases to the private individual, the latter, in this case, can increase the rate of return on the £2000 by placing it with a pension fund.

d) Is the pension fund likely to invest in small manufacturing companies?

6 THE PRICE OF OIL: CAN WE AFFORD IT?

6.1 The world market for oil

Draw a supply and demand curve for world oil $c.1945$ and diagrammatically represent each of the following events with a shift of either the supply, or demand, curve.
a) The increase in output of the Soviet Union and Libya.
b) The US becomes a net importer of oil in 1970.
c) The 6.3% increase in industrial output of OECD countries in 1973.
d) The development of North Sea oil and the Alaska Field.

6.2 The terms of trade

The terms of trade are formally calculated as

$$\frac{\text{index of export prices}}{\text{index of import prices}}\%$$

If the terms of trade shift it will mean either that with a given level of exports a country can afford more imports or that in order to maintain a given level of imports a country will have to export more. To the Western industrial nations the terms of trade can be expressed as:

$$\frac{\text{Index of manufactured product prices}}{\text{Index of raw material prices}}\%$$

a) For what reasons have the terms of trade moved against the Western industrial nations?
b) Why should this shift not be so marked in Britain's case?

6.4 The Keynesian perspective on oil

Make a copy of the Keynesian aggregate demand figure (5). Diagrammatically show how the model is affected by each of the following:

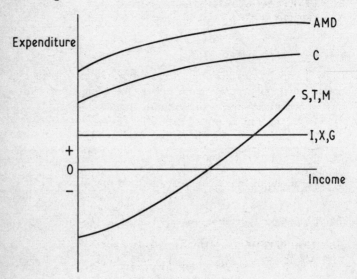

Figure 5

132

a) The effect of a sudden increase in oil prices and the subsequent flows of revenue to the oil exporters.
b) The effect of the restrictive tax and monetary policies which most governments pursued in 1974 in response to the oil price increases.
c) Why did the oil importing countries act in this way, rather than responding to maintain the level of demand?

6.4 World balance of payments

The world as a whole finds itself in the situation which can be roughly represented by the following exercise which assumes a four country world (you can have as many countries as you want but the model works with 4, 40 or 400 so we opt for the simplest). The table shows the international trading position of each of the countries:

Country A

Imports	£	*Exports*	£
Manufactures	100	Oil	250
Surplus	150		
	250		250

Country B

Imports	£	*Exports*	£
Oil	100	Manufactures	150
Manufactures	50	Deficit	50
Raw materials	50		
	200		200

Country C

Imports	£	*Exports*	£
Manufactures	100	Raw materials	100
Oil	50	Deficit	50
	150		150

Country D

Imports	£	Exports	£
Oil	100	Manufactures	150
Manufactures	50	Deficit	50
Raw materials	50		
	200		200

a) What happens if country B devalues its currency in an attempt to make its exports of manufactured products more price attractive in countries A and C?

b) What happens if country D bans all imports of manufactured products from country B?

c) What happens if country A starts to import fifty units of manufactured products from country C instead of importing them from B and D?

d) What would happen if country A reduced the price of oil by 60%?

6.5 Balance of payments and the standard of living

Any country which runs a balance of payments deficit is consuming more goods than it has produced by its own efforts — it does this by borrowing goods from some other country.

Country A, *year 1*

	£		£
Domestic consumption	200	Domestic output	150
		Imports (borrowed output)	50
	200		200

Equally any country which runs a balance of payments surplus is consuming less than it could do, given the level of its own output. It is deliberately under-consuming and lending the surplus output to another country.

Country B, *year 1*

	£		£
Domestic consumption	150	Domestic output	200
Exports (loaned output)	50		
	200		200

In year 2 both countries leave their domestic output at the level it was at in year 1 but country B decides to re-call the output it loaned to country A. Country B has decided to catch up on its level of consumption and wants a domestic consumption level of 250 units this year.

Country B, *year 2*

	£		£
Domestic consumption	250	Domestic output	200
		Imports (reclaimed output)	?
	?		?

What effect will this have upon country A which is now called upon to repay the loan of goods from the previous year?

Country A, *year 2*

	£		£
Domestic consumption	?	Domestic output	150
Exports (repayment output)	?		
	?		?

a) How could the government in country A restrain domestic consumption in year 2 in order to free goods for export?

b) How would the situation be improved for country A if there were unemployed resources in her economy?

c) Has country B improved or lowered its standard of living over the two year period?

d) If the Western industrial nations have been running balance of payments deficits with the oil exporters for some years, what eventually must happen?

135

6.6 Life without oil

Table 13 Foreign trade by principal commodity groups (from OECD Economic Survey of West Germany, May 1980, table G, and OECD Economic Survey of Japan, July 1980, table H)

	West Germany (DM million)	Japan ($m)
Imports		
Food and live animals	30.650	13,683
Beverages and tobacco	3.091	733
Crude materials (inedible) except fuel	23.091	21,842
Mineral fuel, lubricants and related materials	56.729	45,286
Animal and vegetable oils and fats	1.531	354
Chemicals	22.697	5,178
Manufactured goods, chiefly material	54.151	9,411
Machinery and transport equipment	56.372	7,330
Miscellaneous manufactured articles	34.079	5,213
Commodities and transactions not classified according to kind	9.769	1,642
Total imports	292.161	110,672
Exports		
Food and live animals	12.590	1,069
Beverages and tobacco	1.620	138
Crude materials (inedible) except fuel	6.565	1,153
Mineral fuel, lubricants and related materials	10.613	356
Animal and vegetable oils and fats	1.504	115
Chemicals	41.043	6,100
Manufactured goods, chiefly by materials	64.109	26,140
Machinery and transport equipment	141.087	55,284
Miscellaneous manufactured articles	29.325	11,562
Commodities and transactions not classified according to kind	6.164	1,114
Total exports	314.621	103,031

Consider the situation of an oil-less state which has only limited food and raw material resources. A model of its international trading position might be:

Imports	£	Exports	£
Oil	50	Manufactures	150
Food	50		
Raw materials	50		
	150		150

The price of oil is then doubled but the country cannot effect significant reductions in its consumption. Equally it cannot run a persistent balance of payments deficit. What options are open to it?

6.7 Inflation-adjusted price of oil

In year 1 the price of a gallon of petrol is £1.50 and of this 75p goes to the government in duty, 30p goes to the oil producing country in royalty and 45p goes to the oil company. The price level in this country then rises by 10% so the oil company puts up the price of petrol to £1.55 and takes 50p for itself.

a) Relative to other products oil is now cheaper than it was at the start of the year. How much should it cost?
b) By how much should the government raise the duty on petrol to preserve its real price?
c) What has happened to the cost of developing petrol substitutes during the year?
d) What are the long-term implications of not raising the price of petrol to the inflation-adjusted level?

6.8 The impact of a rise in the price of oil

The pattern of consumer expenditure in the UK in the 1970s

was such that the distribution of 100 units of personal disposable income was roughly as follows:

Food	15	Durables	3
Alcohol, drink, tobacco	9	Cars	4
Fuel and light	4	Other goods	14
Housing	12	Other services	18
Clothing	6	Savings	15

If the price of oil now rises so that in the first instance expenditure on fuel must rise to 6%, and on cars to 6%, what options are open to consumers (we know from chapter 5 that they do not see the reduction of savings as an option).

Discuss the view that:

the impact of an oil price increase must either be to create unemployment if consumers are willing to accept a cut in their real incomes or to stimulate inflation if they are not.

Glossary

Balance of payments   The income and expenditure account of a country in its dealings with the rest of the world. It is divided into the current account, which records purchases and sales of goods and services, and the capital account, which records flows of capital: money which is being lent, or invested, or granted. The current account in turn is broken down into two parts: visible and invisible trade. Visible trade is trade in goods, for example, cars, diamonds, and North Sea gas. It covers what we conventionally think of as imports and exports. Invisible trade is more of a ragbag. It includes the payment of interest on loans, the earnings of the City of London from insurance and the expenditure of the overseas tourist who pays to take away the memory of a view of Buckingham Palace.

Capital market   'Markets' in economics are rarely physical places. They are a shorthand term for trading and traders. A capital market is the mechanism for channelling savings into investment, and it is the institutions (such as pension funds and banks) which provide the channel. A foreign exchange market, by analogy, is the mechanism for swapping one country's currency for another, and it is the banks and brokers who carry out the swap.

Cartel   An agreement by a group of people or firms or countries to rig the market in their joint favour. The agreement usually involves restricting supplies of a certain product or commodity in order to drive its price up — or (less often) limiting purchases in order to drive the price down. Producers tend to be better at organizing cartels than consumers, simply because there are usually fewer of them.

Consumption   The using up of goods or services for immediate satisfaction. Economists see only two alternative uses for output. It can be consumed, or it can be invested. Anyone who saves is consciously deciding not to consume. A country which does not consume its entire output is saving resources which are then available for investment, and thus for future economic growth. See also *investment*.

Deflation   Not the opposite of inflation, but a fall in the level of demand within the economy. The opposite is reflation: an expansion of economic activity.

Depreciation   A prolonged tendency for the currency of a country to lose value gradually relative to other currencies. The opposite is appreciation, when a currency rises in value against one or more other currencies.

Eurocurrency   A currency held outside its country of origin. A pound held in a bank account in Germany, or the US, or indeed Timbuktu, is Eurosterling. There are also Eurodollars, Euromarks, Euroyen, and by now perhaps even Eurocowrieshells. Markets in Eurocurrencies, and particularly in the Eurodollar, developed in the 1960s to get round foreign exchange controls. They now represent vast accumulations of internationally mobile funds, uncontrolled by any single monetary authority.

Exchange control   The control by the government of dealings in foreign currency. Examples may range from highly complex restrictions on bank transactions to simple limits on the amount of money that a tourist may take into − or out of − a country. Exchange controls may be intended either to stop people from buying a country's currency (and so driving the exchange rate up) or to stop them from selling (and so driving the exchange rate down).

Exchange rate   The price of one unit of currency in terms of another. Exchange rates are determined by the demand for and supply of a country's currency in the foreign exchange market.

The key exchange rate for most currencies used to be the number of US dollars and cents it would buy. But today, an equally common and useful measure is a weighted average (weighted by the amount of foreign trade of each country) of the currency values of the other main industrial countries.

Exchange reserves   The stock of gold and foreign currency which is held by the central bank to meet its foreign currency debts.

Fiscal policy   Policy involving changes in government spending or taxation. The counterpart is monetary policy, which involves changes in the level of interest rates or in the amount and the way in which the government borrows.

Gross domestic product (GDP)   A measure of the goods and services produced in an economy during a period to time. As people have to be employed to produce these goods and services, GDP is also a measure of income earned. GDP should not be confused with gross national product (GNP) which represents GDP plus income from investments abroad. In the case of Middle Eastern oil states, the difference can be considerable.

Import controls   Limits on the import of goods produced abroad. Import controls come in various forms: tariffs (a tax on imports), quotas (limits on the actual quantity of imports), and import deposits (where the importer has to deposit with the government a proportion of the value of the goods he wants to import).

Inflation   Rising prices – not isolated price increases but a general and persistent tendency for the average price level to rise. Inflation may occur even if the prices of some products are falling; and a fall in the rate of inflation means that prices generally continue to rise but at a slower pace.

Investment   Economists do not use this word as other people do to mean simply money put in a bank or into a holding of shares). Properly used, investment is the purchase of goods or the allocation of time to ensure a future flow of goods or services. It implies a certain durability. For a government, building a house or a nuclear power station is investment; buying a soldier's uniform or paying a teacher's wage is not. For a company, buying a van or building a factory is investment (buildings are usually described as 'plant' in this context). Investment is an inevitable prerequisite for, and consequence of, faster economic growth.

Multinational   A company which has substantial operations in more than one country.

Nationalized industry   An industry which is largely or wholly owned by the public sector.

National debt   The accumulated borrowings of the public sector, past and present.

Opportunity cost   The cost of taking one course of action measured in terms of the benefit which would have been derived from taking another. Time spent reading this book could have been spent watching television. As time, like all other resources, is in limited supply, one of the key economic problems for individuals and society is how to choose courses of action which give the greatest possible benefit for the lowest possible cost.

Primary products   Unprocessed or unmanufactured goods, for example foodstuffs, fuel and raw materials, for industrial production. Coal, bananas and iron ore are all primary products. Most developing countries earn their livings by selling primary products to the industrialized countries − although some industrial countries (notably the US, the USSR, Australia, and Canada) are large producers of primary products.

Public goods   Goods which cannot be consumed by one person without their giving benefit to others upon whom there is no charge levied for the benefit received. Hence the goods are provided communally, for example defence, law and order, roads, education(?), health(?).

Public sector   That part of the economy directly controlled by the government. It includes central government (the armed forces, law courts, etc.), local government (education, council housing, etc.), public corporations like the BBC, and nationalized industries like British Rail and the Post Office.

Real Any quantity given in 'real' terms is measured against the amount of goods and services it will buy. By contrast, a quantity in 'nominal' terms is measured in cash, and will rise if prices rise even if the actual quantity of goods and services involved remains unchanged. To take one example: nominal wages are measured in the pounds and pence of the day when they are paid. Comparing your nominal wage last year with that of today says nothing about your living standards. But real wages are measured in terms of purchasing power. So a 'real' measure — of income, output, expenditure or whatever — is one which attempts to strip inflation out of the picture, and to see what is happening to the quantities, the volumes, involved.

Recession A period when the level of demand in the economy falls behind the growth of capacity. The result is unused resources: unemployment, idle machinery, empty factories, etc.

Standard of living Economists tend to use gross national product per head as a measure of the standard of living. That is a way of using the availability of goods and services per head of population to judge how well off people are. Some would argue that GNP per head is a bad measure of the standard of living, because GNP only includes those goods and services which can be valued. It excludes clean air, family life, low crime and culture. This argument tends to surface particularly at times when the growth of GNP is slow.

Terms of trade The ratio of export prices to import prices. If export prices rise faster than import prices, then the terms of trade are said to improve, or to move in a country's favour. The effect is to leave the country better off, since it can buy more imports for the same volume of exports.

Transfer payment Not, in economics, a fee for wandering footballers but a payment which is made to redistribute income between individuals, or between individuals and companies. Examples are student grants, state pensions, unemployment benefit, regional aid, or pocket money. Transfer payments are not made in return for the production of goods and services. They therefore are not included in the calculation of GDP. This is why — *pace* Margaret Thatcher — it would be perfectly possible to have an economy in which public expenditure represented 100% of GDP — if everyone paid everything they earned in taxation, and received it all back in the form of a state benefit.

Velocity Money circulates in the economy when it moves from one wallet — or one bank account — to another. The velocity, or speed, with which this happens may change over time. Imagine what must have happened when the credit card was invented. The faster a given supply of money circulates, the more transactions it can be used to finance.

References and bibliography

Texts marked with an asterisk (*) are suggested introductory reading.

General

Brittan, Samuel (1969) *Steering the Economy* (London: Secker & Warburg).

Caves, R. E. (1968) *Britain's Economic Prospects* (Washington, DC: The Brookings Institution; available in the UK from Basil Blackwell).

* Caves, R. E. and Krause, Lawrence, B. (eds) (1980) *Britain's Economic Performance* (Washington, DC: The Brookings Institution; available in the UK from Basil Blackwell).

Donaldson, Peter (1970) *Guide to the British Economy* (Harmondsworth: Penguin).

* Galbraith, J. K. and Salinger, Nicole (1981) *Almost Everyone's Guide to Economics* (Harmondsworth: Penguin).

* Hutton, John (1978) *The Mystery of Wealth* (Cheltenham: Stanley Thornes).

* Morris, Derek (ed.) (1979) *The Economic System in the UK* (Oxford: Oxford University Press).

* Trevithick, J. A. (1977) *Inflation: A Guide to the Crisis in Economics* (Harmondsworth: Penguin).

Chapter 1

Allsopp, C. and Joshi, V. (1980) 'Alternative strategies for the

UK', *The National Institute of Economic and Social Research Economic Review*, February, pp. 86–104.

Blackaby, Frank (ed.) (1972) *An Incomes Policy for Britain* (London: Heinemann).

Economic Trends Annual Supplement (1980) (London: HMSO).

Friedman, M. (1970) *The Counter-Revolution in Monetary Theory*, occasional paper no. 33 (London: Institute of Economic Affairs).

Friedman, Milton and Friedman, Rose (1980) *Free to Choose: A Personal Statement* (London: Secker & Warburg).

Gould, Bryan, Mills, John and Stewart, Shaun (1981) *Monetarism or Prosperity* (London: Macmillan).

* House of Commons Treasury and Civil Service Committee (1980) *Report on Monetary Policy* (House of Commons paper 163–1); and *Memoranda on Monetary Policy*, vols I & II (House of Commons papers 720, 720–II) (London: HMSO).

Keynes, John Maynard (1936; 2nd ed. 1963) *The General Theory of Employment, Interest and Money* (London: Macmillan).

Mill, John Stuart (1948; 1965) *Principles of Political Economy* (London: Routledge & Kegan Paul).

Posner, Michael (ed.) (1978) *Demand Management* (London: Heinemann and the National Institute of Economic and Social Research).

* Stewart, Michael (1970) *Keynes and After* (Harmondsworth: Penguin).

Chapter 2

Cairncross, A. K. (1971) *Essays in Economic Management* (London: Allen & Unwin).

Clarke, Richard (1978) *Public Expenditure, Management and Control* (London: Macmillan).

Economic Trends, May (1980) (London: HMSO).

* Else, P. K. and Marshall, G. (1979) *The Management of Public Expenditure* (Policy Studies Institute Report 580).

Friedman, Milton and Friedman, Rose (1980) *Free to Choose: A Personal Statement* (London: Secker & Warburg).

Goldman, Samuel (1973) *The Developing System of Public Expenditure Management and Control* (Civil Service College Studies No. 2).

Heclo, H. and Wildavsky, Aaron (1974) *The Private Government of Public Money* (London: Macmillan).

National Income and Expenditure (Blue Book) (1980) (London: HMSO).

Seldon, Arthur (ed.) (1976) *The Dilemmas of Government Expenditure* (London: Institute of Economic Affairs).

Seldon, Arthur (1977) *Charge* (London: Temple Smith).

Robinson, A. (1978) *Parliament and Public Spending* (London: Heinemann).

The Treasury (1978) *Public Expenditure: Economic Progress Report*, October (available from Central Office of Information, see p. 127).

* Wright, Maurice (1981) *Public Spending Decisions* (London: Allen & Unwin).

Chapter 3

Armstrong, W. (1980) *Budgetary Reform in the UK* (Oxford: Oxford University Press).

Brown, C. V. and Jackson, P. M. (1978) *Public Sector Economics* (Oxford: Martin Robertson).

Hansard (1981) *House of Commons Debates*, 19 February (London: HMSO).

* Kay, John and King, Melvyn (1978; 2nd ed. 1980). *The British Tax System* (Oxford: Oxford University Press).

McClements, Leslie (1978) *The Economics of Social Security* (London: Heinemann).

Meade, James (1978) *The Structure and Reform of Direct Taxation* (London: Allen & Unwin).

National Consumer Council (1979) *The Consumer and the State* (London: National Consumer Council).

Royal Commission on the Distribution of Income and Wealth − report no. 7 (Cmnd 6626) and report no. 8 (Cmnd 7679) (London: HMSO).

Chapter 4

Bacon, Robert and Eltis, Walter (2nd ed. 1978) *Britain's Economic Problems: Too Few Producers* (London: Macmillan).

* Blackaby, Frank (ed.) (1979) *De-industrialization* (London:

Heinemann and National Institute of Economic and Social Research).

Cambridge Economic Policy Reviews (1981) *Economic Policy in the UK*, April (vol. 7, no. 1) (Farnborough: Gower).

Economic Trends (1981) no. 331, May (London: HMSO).

Gould, Bryan, Mills, John and Stewart, Shaun (1981) *Monetary or Prosperity* (London: Macmillan).

Hutton, John (1978) *The Mystery of Wealth* (Cheltenham: Stanley Thornes).

Institute of Economic Affairs (1979) *Over-ruled on Welfare* (London: Institute of Economic Affairs).

King, Melvyn (1975) 'The UK profits crisis: myth or reality?', *Economic Journal*, March (vol. 85, no. 337), pp. 33–54.

OECD (1980) *Tourism Policy and International Tourism in OECD Member Countries* (Paris: OECD).

Rostow, W. W. (1959; 2nd ed. 1971) *Stages of Economic Growth* (Cambridge: Cambridge University Press).

Chapter 5

Building Societies Association (1981) *Building Societies in 1980* (London: Building Societies Association).

* Clarke, William (1979) *Inside the City* (London: Allen & Unwin).

Committee to Review the Functioning of the Financial Institutions (1980) Report vol. I, vol. II appendices (Cmnd 7937) (London: HMSO).

Economic Trends Annual Supplement (1981) (London: HMSO).

Lipsey, R. G. (5th ed. 1975) *An Introduction to Positive Economics* (London: Weidenfeld & Nicolson).

* McRae, Hamish and Cairncross, Frances (1974) *Capital City: London as a Financial Centre* (London: Eyre Methuen).

Shaw, E. R. (1975) *The London Money Market* (London: Heinemann).

Chapter 6

Bank of England (1980) 'The surpluses of the oil exporters', *Bank of England Quarterly Bulletin*, June, pp. 154–9.

Cairncross, Frances and McRae, Hamish (1975) *The Second Great Crash* (London: Methuen).

Fried, Edward and Schultze, Charles (eds) (1975) *Higher Oil Prices and the World Economy: Adjustment Problem* (Washington, DC: The Brookings Institution; available in the UK from Basil Blackwell).

* OECD (1980) 'The impact of oil on the world economy', *Economic Outlook*, July, pp. 114–30.

'The world economic crisis' (1980) (London: The Commonwealth Secretariat).

Acknowledgements

The authors and publishers would like to thank the following for permission to reproduce copyright material:

The Guardian and Iain Guest for an extract from an article that appeared 20 May 1981; *The Times* and Lord Nicholas Kaldor for an extract from an article that appeared 6 August 1980; the Controller of Her Majesty's Stationery Office for Tables 1, 2, 8 and 10.